QUICK & EASY
Spanish

learn the basics with the easy-to-follow CD and book

QUICK & EASY spanish

City guide compiled by Rob Alcraft
Translations by The ASK Group Ltd
Map by Hardlines

Published by Top That! Publishing plc
Tide Mill Way, Woodbridge, Suffolk, IP12 IAP, UK
www.topthatpublishing.com
Copyright © 2011 Top That! Publishing plc
All rights reserved
4 6 8 9 7 5 3
Printed and bound in China

CONTENTS

Introduction	3	Eating Out	30
Pronunciation guide	4	Business	35
Everyday Spanish	5	Shopping	39
Numbers	8	Nightlife	45
Time, Dates and Seasons	9	Health	48
Money	10	Emergencies	52
Post	11	City Essentials	54
Telephones	12	Getting Around	55
Directions	14	Things to see and do	58
Travel	15	Museums and Galleries	62
Staying the Night	21	Enjoying Madrid	63
Leisure and Sport	27		

QUICK AND EASY SPANISH

Visiting a new country is always exciting but basic language barriers can be a problem. Designed to give you a command of basic phrases, this Quick and Easy Language guide will make communicating in another language simple, enabling you to ask for what you need in everyday situations and understand other people's responses.

Each English phrase is given with its Spanish equivalent, and a guide to pronunciation. The book is arranged in easy reference sections, and you can use it as an on-the-spot reminder. Accompanying the book is a CD containing 200 essential phrases so that you can learn some of the basics before you go, and gain confidence in your pronunciation.

With the worries of communication out of the way you can be free to enjoy your stay. To help make the most of it you can use the handy city guide at the back of this book which includes tips for getting around Madrid and the best attractions that shouldn't be missed.

PRONUNCIATION GUIDE

If you have difficulty pronouncing any of the Spanish words, simply look up the sound you are having difficulty with, in this table. Alongside each Spanish sound there is an English word containing a similar sound. Alternatively, use the CD and learn the phrases marked with the CD symbol.

SPANISH SOUND	LETTERS USED IN TRANSLITERATION	PRONOUNCED AS IN ENGLISH WORD
c (when followed by 'e' or 'i')	th	thumb
d (when at end of certain words)	th	thumb
g (before 'e' and 'i' - a sound made at the back of the throat)	kh	loch
g (followed by 'ua')	gw	gwent
h (generally silent – some exceptions when part of other sounds)		
j (a sound made at the back of the throat)	kh	loch
ll	y	yes
ñ	ny	onion
qu	k	kite
rr (a rolled 'r')	rr	(no equivalent)
v (generally this is pronounced as 'b', although in some cases, such as 'por favor', the sound is more like a 'v')	b	baby

04 PRONUNCIATION GUIDE

EVERYDAY SPANISH

BASIC PHRASES

English	Spanish	Pronunciation
🔊 Yes.	Sí.	See.
🔊 No.	No.	Noh.
🔊 Thank you.	Gracias.	Grah-thee-ahs.
Ok.	Vale.	Bah-leh.
🔊 Hi.	Buenas.	Bweh-nahs.
🔊 Hello.	Hola.	Oh-lah.
🔊 Goodbye.	Adiós.	Ahd-ee-ohs.
🔊 Good, great.	Bien, estupendo.	Bee-ehn, est-oo-pend-oh.
🔊 That's fine.	Está bien.	Ehs-tah bee-ehn.
That's right.	Es correcto.	Ehs koh-rrekt-oh.
🔊 Good morning.	Buenos días.	Bweh-nohs dee-ahs.
🔊 Good afternoon.	Buenas tardes.	Bweh-nahs tahr-dehs.
🔊 Goodnight.	Buenas noches.	Bweh-nahs noch-ehs.
🔊 I don't understand.	No entiendo.	Noh ehn-tee-ehn-doh
🔊 What does this mean?	¿Qué significa esto?	¿Keh seeg-nee-fee-kah ehs-toh?
See you later.	Hasta luego.	Ahs-tah lweh-goh.
🔊 Pleased to meet you.	Encantado de conocerle.	Ehn-kahn-tah-doh deh kohn-oh-thehr-leh.
🔊 How are you?	¿Cómo está?	¿Koh-moh ehs-tah?
🔊 I'm very well, thanks.	Muy bien, gracias.	Mwee bee-ehn, grah-thee-ahs.
What's your name?	¿Cómo se llama?	¿Koh-moh seh yah-mah?
This is my husband.	Éste es mi marido.	Ehs-teh ehs mee mah-ree-doh.
This is my wife.	Ésta es mi mujer.	Ehs-tah ehs mee moo-khehr.
This is my son.	Éste es mi hijo.	Ehs-teh ehs mee ee-khoh.
This is my daughter.	Ésta es mi hija.	Ehs-tah ehs mee ee-khah.
This is my colleague.	Éste/a es mi colega.	Ehs-teh/tah ehs mee koh-leh-gah.
🔊 Excuse me.	Disculpe.	Dees-kool-peh.
🔊 Do you speak English?	¿Habla inglés?	¿Ah-blah eeng-lehs?
Could you say that again?	¿Podría repetirlo?	¿Pohd-ree-ah reh-peh-teer-loh?
🔊 Can you speak more slowly?	¿Podría hablar más despacio?	¿Pohd-ree-ah ahb-lahr mahs dehs-path-ee-oh?
Please can you write it down for me?	¿Me lo podría escribir, por favor?	¿Meh loh pohd-ree-ah ehsk-ree-beer, pohr fah-vohr?
Can you help me please?	¿Puede ayudarme, por favor?	¿Pweh-deh ah-yoo-dahr-meh, pohr fah-vohr?

🔊 = Phrase featured on the CD

EVERYDAY SPANISH 05

ABOUT YOU

My name is…	Me llamo…	Meh yah-moh…
I'm married.	Estoy casado (M) /casada (F)	Ehs-toy kah-sah-doh /kah-sah-da
I'm not married	No estoy casado (M) /casada (F)	Noh ehs-toy kah-sah-doh /kah-sah-dah.
I have… children.	Tengo… hijos.	Tehng-oh… ee-khos.
I live in…	Vivo en…	Bee-boh ehn…
I'm staying at…	Me alojo en…	Meh ah-loh-khoh en…
I'm on holiday.	Estoy de vacaciones.	Ehs-toy deh bah-kah-thee-oh-nehs.
I'm here on business.	Estoy aquí por negocios.	Ehs-toy ah-kee pohr neh-goh-thee-ohs.
I'm here for…	Estaré aquí…	Ehs-tahr-reh ah-kee…
/days.	/días.	/dee-ahs.
/weeks.	/semanas.	/seh-mahn-ahs.
I've come from…	He venido de…	Eh beh-nee-doh deh…
I'm going to…	Voy a…	Boy ah…

HEARING

Can I help you?	¿Puedo ayudarle?	¿Pweh-doh ah-yoo-dahr-leh?
What do you want?	¿Qué desea?	¿Keh deh-seh-ah?
What are you looking for?	¿Qué está buscando?	¿Keh ehs-tah boos-kahn-doh?
What is your name?	¿Cómo se llama?	¿Koh-moh seh yah-mah?
Have you booked?	¿Ha reservado?	¿Ah reh-sehr-bah-doh?

BASIC REQUESTS

I WANT

I want…	Quisiera…	Kee-see-ehr-ah…
/a room.	/una habitación.	/ooh-nah ahb-ee-tath-ee-ohn.
/a drink.	/una bebida.	/ooh-nah beh-bee-dah.
/something to eat.	/algo para comer.	/ahl-goh pah-rah kohm-ehr.

EVERYDAY SPANISH

WHAT?

What is the time?	¿Qué hora es?	¿Keh-oh-rah ehs?
What is your name?	¿Cómo se llama?	¿Koh-moh seh yah-mah?
What is the problem?	¿Cuál es el problema?	¿Kwahl ehs ehl proh-bleh-mah?

WHERE?

Where is...	¿Dónde está...	¿Dohn-deh ehs-tah...
/the bank?	/el banco?	/ehl bahn-koh?
/the park?	/el parque?	/ehl pahr-keh?

WHEN?

When...	¿Cuándo...	¿Kwahn-doh...
/does the film start?	/empieza la película?	/ehm-pee-eth-ah lah peh-lee-koo-lah?
/does the gallery open?	/abre la galería?	/ahb-reh lah gah-leh-ree-ah?

HOW?

How much is it?	¿Cuánto cuesta?	¿Kwahn-toh kwehs-tah?
How do I get there?	¿Cómo puedo llegar hasta allí?	¿Koh-moh pweh-doh yeh-gahr ahs-tah ah-yee?

CONTRASTS

It is...	Es/está...	Ehs/ehs-tah...
good/bad	bueno/malo	bweh-noh/mah-loh
big/small	grande/pequeño	grahn-deh/peh-keh-nyoh
high/low	alto/bajo	ahl-toh/bah-khoh
expensive/cheap	caro/barato	kah-roh/bah-rah-toh
busy/empty	lleno/vacío	yeh-noh/bah-thee-oh
old/new	viejo/nuevo	bee-eh-khoh/nweh-boh
fast/slow	rápido/lento	rah-pee-doh/lehn-toh
quiet/noisy	tranquilo/ruidoso	trahn-keel-oh/roo-ee-dohs-soh
hot/cold	caliente/frío	kah-lee-ehn-teh/free-oh
open/shut	abierto/cerrado	ahb-ee-ehr-toh/theh-rrah-doh
interesting/boring	interesante/aburrido	een-teh-reh-sahn-teh/ahb-oh-rree-doh
I like it.	Me gusta.	Meh goos-tah.
I don't like it.	No me gusta.	Noh meh goos-tah.

EVERYDAY SPANISH

NUMBERS

🔊 one	**uno**	ooh-noh
🔊 two	**dos**	dohs
🔊 three	**tres**	trehs
🔊 four	**cuatro**	kwah-troh
🔊 five	**cinco**	theen-koh
🔊 six	**seis**	seh-ees
🔊 seven	**siete**	see-eh-teh
🔊 eight	**ocho**	oh-choh
🔊 nine	**nueve**	nweh-beh
🔊 ten	**diez**	dee-eth
🔊 eleven	**once**	ohn-theh
🔊 twelve	**doce**	doh-theh
🔊 thirteen	**trece**	treh-theh
🔊 fourteen	**catorce**	kah-tohr-theh
🔊 fifteen	**quince**	keen-theh
🔊 sixteen	**dieciséis**	dee-eth-ee-seh-ees
🔊 seventeen	**diecisiete**	dee-eth-ee-see-eh-teh
🔊 eighteen	**dieciocho**	dee-eth-ee-oh-choh
🔊 nineteen	**diecinueve**	dee-eth-ee-nweh-beh
🔊 twenty	**veinte**	beh-een-teh
🔊 twenty-one	**veintiuno**	beh-een-tee-ooh-noh
🔊 twenty-two	**veintidós**	beh-een-tee-dohs
🔊 thirty	**treinta**	treh-een-tah
🔊 thirty-one	**treinta y uno**	treh-een-tah ee ooh-noh
🔊 thirty-two	**treinta y dos**	treh-een-tah ee dohs
🔊 forty	**cuarenta**	kwah-rehn-tah
🔊 fifty	**cincuenta**	theen-kwehn-tah
🔊 sixty	**sesenta**	seh-sehn-tah
🔊 seventy	**setenta**	seh-tehn-tah
🔊 eighty	**ochenta**	oh-chehn-tah
🔊 ninety	**noventa**	noh-behn-tah
🔊 one hundred	**cien**	thee-ehn
one hundred and ten	**ciento diez**	thee-ehn-toh dee-eth
one hundred and twenty	**ciento veinte**	thee-ehn-toh beh-een-teh
five hundred	**quinientos**	keen-ee-ehn-tohs
one thousand	**mil**	meel
five thousand	**cinco mil**	theen-koh meel
one million	**un millón**	oon meel-yohn

08 NUMBERS

TIME, DATES AND SEASONS

today	hoy	oy
tonight	esta noche	ehs-tah noh-cheh
this morning	esta mañana	ehs-tah mah-nyah-nah
tomorrow morning	mañana por la mañana	mah-nyah-nah pohr lah mah-nyah-nah
this afternoon	esta tarde	ehs-tah tahr-deh
tomorrow afternoon	mañana por la tarde	mah-nyah-nah pohr lah tahr-deh
this evening	esta noche	ehs-tah noh-cheh
tomorrow evening	mañana por la noche	mah-nyah-nah pohr lah noh-cheh
midday	mediodía	meh-dee-oh-dee-ah
midnight	medianoche	meh-dee-ah-noh-cheh
yesterday	ayer	ah-yehr
this week	esta semana	ehs-tah seh-mahn-ah
next week	la semana que viene	lah seh-mahn-ah keh bee-ehn-neh
later on	más tarde	mahs tahr-deh
hour	hora	oh-rah
four o'clock	cuatro en punto	kwah-troh ehn poon-toh
half past	y media	ee meh-dee-ah
half past four	cuatro y media	kwah-troh ee meh-dee-ah
quarter past	y cuarto	ee kwahr-toh
quarter past ten	diez y cuarto	dee-eth ee kwahr-toh
quarter to	menos cuarto	meh-nohs kwahr-toh
quarter to five	cinco menos cuarto	theen-koh meh-nohs kwahr-toh

DATES AND SEASONS

1st March	uno de marzo	ooh-noh deh mahr-thoh
January	enero	eh-nehr-roh
February	febrero	feh-brehr-roh
March	marzo	mahr-thoh
April	abril	ahb-reel
May	mayo	mah-yoh
June	junio	khooh-nee-oh
July	julio	khooh-lee-oh
August	agosto	ah-gohs-toh
September	septiembre	sehp-tee-ehm-breh
October	octubre	ohk-tooh-breh
November	noviembre	noh-bee-ehm-breh
December	diciembre	dee-thee-ehm-breh
Spring	primavera	pree-mah-behr-ah
Summer	verano	behr-ahn-oh
Autumn	otoño	oh-toh-nyoh
Winter	invierno	een-bee-ehr-noh

MONEY

English	Spanish	Pronunciation
Where is the nearest bank?	¿Dónde está el banco más cercano?	¿Dohn-deh ehs-tah ehl bahn-koh mahs thehr-kahn-oh?
When does the bank open?	¿Cuándo abre el banco?	¿Kwahn-doh ahb-reh ehl bahn-koh?
Is there a cash point near here?	¿Hay un cajero automático cerca de aquí?	¿I oon kah-khehr-oh ow-toh-maht-ee-koh thehr-kah deh ah-kee?
Where can I cash these traveller's cheques?	¿Dónde puedo cambiar cheques de viaje?	¿Dohn-deh pweh-doh kahm-bee-ahr cheh-kehs deh bee-ah-kheh?
What is the exchange rate?	¿Cuál es el tipo de cambio?	¿Kwahl ehs ehl tee-poh deh kahm-bee-oh?
Could I have some smaller notes please?	¿Podría darme billetes más pequeños, por favor?	¿Pohd-dree-ah dahr-meh beel-yeh-tehs mahs peh-keh-nyos, pohr fah-vohr?
Could I have some coins please?	¿Podría darme monedas, por favor?	¿Pohd-dree-ah dahr-meh mohn-neh-dahs, pohr fah-vohr?

HEARING

English	Spanish	Pronunciation
Can I see...	¿Podría mostrarme...	¿Pohd-ree-ah mohs-trah-meh
/some identification?	/alguna identificación?	/ahl-goon-ah ee-den-tee-fee-kak-thee-ohn?
/your passport?	/su pasaporte?	/sooh pah-sah-pohr-teh?
/your card?	/su tarjeta?	/sooh tahr-kheh-tah?
How much do you want?	¿Cuánto quiere?	¿Kwahn-toh kee-ehr-eh?
Please sign here.	Firme aquí, por favor.	Feer-meh ah-kee, pohr fah-vohr.
What's your address here?	¿Cuál es su dirección aquí?	¿Kwahl ehs sooh dee-rehk-thee-ohn ah-kee?

PROBLEMS

The machine has eaten my card.	El cajero se ha tragado mi tarjeta.	Ehl kah-khehr-roh seh ah trah-gah-doh mee tahr-heh-tah.
My card won't work.	Mi tarjeta no funciona.	Mee tahr-kheht-tah noh foon-thee-ohn-ah.
Could I check my balance?	¿Podría ver mi saldo?	¿Pohd-ree-ah behr mee sahl-doh?
Can you call my bank?	¿Podría llamar a mi banco?	¿Pohd-ree-ah yah-mahr ah mee bahn-koh?

MONEY

POST

USEFUL WORDS

English	Spanish	Pronunciation
all transactions	todas las transacciones	tohd-ahs lahs trahn-sahk-thee-ohn-ehs
bank	banco	bahn-koh
buy	comprar	kohm-prahr
cash desk	caja	kah-khah
cash machine	cajero automático	kah-khehr-oh ow-toh-maht-ee-koh
cashier	cajero	kah-khehr-oh
charge	cobrar	kohb-rahr
closed	cerrado	theh-rrah-doh
commission	comisión	kohm-ees-ee-ohn
credit card	tarjeta de crédito	tahr-kheh-ta deh kreh-dee-toh
deposit	ingreso	een-greh-soh
identification	identificación	ee-dehn-tee-fee-kah-thee-ohn
exchange rate	tipo de cambio	tee-poh deh kahm-bee-oh
form	impreso	eem-preh-soh
money	dinero	dee-nehr-oh
notes	billetes	beel-yeh-tehs
open	abierto	ahb-ee-ehr-toh
pounds sterling	libras esterlinas	leeb-rahs ehs-tehr-lee-nahs
withdrawal	retirada de dinero	reh-tee-rah-dah deh dee-nehr-oh

English	Spanish	Pronunciation
Can I have stamps for postcards to the UK?	Quiero sellos para mandar postales al Reino Unido	Kee-ehr-oh sehl-yohs pah-rah mahn-dahr pohs-tahl-ehs ahl Reh-ee-noh Ooh-nee-doh
Where can I post this?	¿Dónde puedo mandar esto por correo?	¿Dohn-deh pweh-doh mahn-dahr ehs-toh pohr koh-rreh-oh?
Where can I buy stamps?	¿Dónde puedo comprar sellos?	¿Dohn-deh pweh-doh kohm-prahr sehl-yohs?
Do you sell stamps?	¿Venden sellos?	¿Behn-dehn sehl-yohs?
Do you sell postcards?	¿Venden postales?	¿Behn-dehn pohs-tahl-ehs?
How much to send this letter/parcel to the USA?	¿Cuánto cuesta mandar esta carta/este paquete a Estados Unidos?	¿Kwahn-toh kwehs-tah mahn-dahr ehs-tah cahr-tah/ehs-teh pah-keh-teh ah Ehs-tahd-dohs Ooh-nee-dohs?
I want to send this to Ireland.	Quiero mandar esto a Irlanda.	Kee-ehr-oh mahn-dahr ehs-toh ah Eer-lahn-dah.

MONEY AND POST 11

TELEPHONES

Is there a public telephone here?	¿Hay un teléfono público por aquí?	¿I oon teh-leh-foh-noh poob-lee-koh pohr ah-kee?
May I use your telephone?	¿Puedo utilizar su teléfono?	¿Pweh-doh oo-tee-lee-thahr soo teh-leh-foh-noh?
Where can I buy a phone card?	¿Dónde puedo comprar una tarjeta de teléfono?	¿Dohn-deh pweh-doh kohm-prahr ooh-na tahr-kheh-ta deh teh-leh-foh-noh?
Do you have change for the telephone?	¿Tiene cambio para el teléfono?	¿Tee-eh-neh kahm-bee-oh pah-rah ehl teh-leh-foh-noh?
What is the telephone number here?	¿Cuál es el número de teléfono de aquí?	¿Kwahl ehs ehl noo-mehr-oh deh teh-leh-foh-noh deh ah-kee?
What number do I call to get directory enquiries?	¿Qué número tengo que marcar para información telefónica?	¿Keh noo-mehr-oh tehn-goh keh mahr-kahr pah-rah een-fohr-mah-thee-ohn teh-leh-fohn-nee-kah?
Can you repeat that?	¿Me lo podría repetir?	¿Meh loh pohd-ree-ah reh-peh-teer?

HEARING

Who's speaking?	¿Quién es?	¿Kee-ehn ehs?
What is your name?	¿Cómo se llama usted?	¿Kohm-oh seh yah-mah oos-teth?
I'll put you through.	Le paso.	Leh pah-soh.
They're not here.	No están.	Noh ehs-tahn.
Can you call back?	¿Puede llamar más tarde?	¿Pweh-deh yah-mahr mahs tahr-deh?
Can I take a message?	¿Quiere dejar un mensaje?	¿Kee-ehr-eh deh-khahr oon mehn-sah-heh?

USEFUL WORDS

call box	Cabina	kahb-een-ah
change	cambio	kahm-bee-oh
dial	marcar	mahr-kahr
engaged	comunicando	koh-moo-nee-kahn-doh
form	impreso	eem-preh-soh
letter	carta	kahr-tah
number	número	noo-mehr-oh
operator	operadora	oh-pehr-ah-doh-rah
parcel	paquete	pah-keh-teh
place	lugar	loo-gahr
postcode	código postal	koh-dee-koh pohs-tahl

12 TELEPHONES

MAKING A CALL

- Can I speak to...? — ¿Puedo hablar con...? — ¿Pweh-doh ahb-lahr kohn...?
- When will they be back? — ¿Cuándo volverán? — ¿Kwahn-doh bohl-behr-ahn?
- Can you ask them to call me, please? — Dígales que me llamen, por favor. — Dee-gah-lehs keh meh yah-mehn, pohr fah-vohr.
- I don't speak much Spanish, can you speak English? — No hablo bien español, ¿Habla inglés? — Noh ahb-loh bee-ehn ehs-pah-nyohl, ¿Ahb-blah eeng-lehs?
- Can you say that again, please? — ¿Me lo podría repetir, por favor? — ¿Meh loh pohd-ree-ah reh-peh-teer, pohr fah-vohr?
- Hold on a moment, please. — Un momento, por favor. — Oon moh-mehn-toh, pohr fah-vohr.
- I will call later. — Llamaré más tarde. — Yah-mah-reh mahs tahr-deh.
- Can I reverse the charges? — ¿Puedo llamar a cobro revertido? — ¿Pweh-doh yah-mahr ah koh-broh reh-behr-tee-doh

TELEPHONES 13

DIRECTIONS

Where is the nearest... ?	¿Dónde está el (la)...más cercano(a)?	¿Dohn-deh ehs-tah ehl (lah)... mahs thehr-kahn-oh(ah)?
How do I get to... ?	¿Cómo puedo ir a... ?	¿Koh-moh pweh-doh eer ah... ?
Can you show me where we are on this map, please?	Por favor, ¿podría señalarme en el plano dónde estamos?	Pohr fah-vohr, ¿pohd-ree-ah seh-nyah-lahr-meh ehn ehl plah-noh dohn-deh ehs-tahm-ohs?
I'm lost.	Me he perdido.	Meh eh pehr-dee-doh.
I need to get to...	Tengo que ir a...	Tehn-goh keh eer ah...
Can you help me please?	¿Puede ayudarme, por favor?	¿Pweh-deh ah-yoo-dah-meh, pohr fah-vohr?

HEARING

You're going the wrong way.	Va por el camino equivocado.	Bah pohr ehl kah-mee-noh eh-kee-boh-kah-doh.
Where are you going?	¿Adónde va?	¿Ah-dohn-deh bah?
Keep going this way.	Siga por aquí.	See-gah pohr ah-kee.
Go left.	Gire a la izquierda.	Khee-reh ah lah eeth-kee-ehr-dah.
Go right.	Gire a la derecha.	Khee-reh ah lah deh-reh-chah.
Go straight on.	Siga recto.	See-gah rehk-toh.
I'll take you there.	Yo le llevo hasta allí.	Yoh leh yeh-boh ahs-tah ah-yee.
Over there.	Allí.	Ah-yee.

USEFUL WORDS

alley	callejón	kah-yeh-khohn
bridge	puente	pwehn-teh
building	edificio	eh-dee-fee-thee-oh
door	puerta	pwehr-tah
entrance	entrada	ehn-trah-dah
gate	puerta	pwehr-tah
left	izquierda	eeth-kee-ehr-dah
lift	ascensor	ahs-then-sohr
museum	museo	moo-seh-oh
right	derecha	deh-reh-chah
shopping mall	centro comercial	thehn-troh kohm-ehr-thee-ahl
signposted	señalado	seh-nyal-ah-doh
square	plaza	plah-thah
straight	recto	rekt-oh
street	calle	kahl-yeh
tower	torre	toh-rreh
wall	muro	moo-roh

14 DIRECTIONS

TRAVEL

HEARING

When do you want to leave/travel?
¿Cuándo quiere salir/viajar?
¿Kwahn-doh kee-ehr-eh sah-leer/bee-ah-khar?

How many people are travelling?
¿Cuánta gente va a viajar?
¿Kwahn-tah khehn-teh bah ah bee-ah-khahr?

There's no train/bus today.
Hoy no hay ningún tren/autobús.
Oy noh I neen-goon trehn/ow-toh-boos.

It's leaving now.
Sale ahora mismo.
Sah-leh ah-ohr-ah mees-moh.

... ON THE BUS

Where can I catch the bus to... ?
¿Dónde puedo tomar el autobús a... ?
¿Dohn-deh pweh-doh tohm-ahr ehl ow-toh-boos ah... ?

What number bus should I catch for... ?
¿Qué autobús debería tomar para ir a... ?
¿Keh ow-toh-boos deh-beh-ree-ah tohm-ahr pah-rah eer ah... ?

Do you know when the next bus is?
¿Sabe usted a qué hora llega el próximo autobús?
¿Sahb-eh oos-teth ah keh oh-rah yeh-gah ehl prohk-see-moh ow-toh-boos?

Can you tell me how often they run?
¿Con qué frecuencia salen?
¿Kon keh freh-kwen-thee-ah sah-lehn?

Can I buy a ticket on the bus?
¿Puedo comprar el billete en el autobús?
¿Pweh-doh kohm-prahr ehl beel-yeh-teh ehn ehl ow-toh-boos?

How much is the fare to... ?
¿Cuánto cuesta el billete para...?
¿Kwahn-toh kwehs-tah ehl beel-yeh-teh pah-rah...?

Can you tell me when to get off?
¿Me podría avisar cuando lleguemos a mi parada?
¿Meh pohd-ree-ah ah-bee-sahr kwahn-doh yeh-geh-mohs ah mee pah-rah-dah?

Does this bus go to... ?
¿Este autobús va a... ?
¿Ehs-teh ow-toh-boos bah ah...?

... METRO AND TAXI

Where is the nearest metro station?
¿Dónde está la estación de metro más cercana?
¿Dohn-deh ehs-tah lah ehs-tah-thee-ohn deh meh-troh mahs thehr-kahn-ah?

Where can I get a metro map?
¿Dónde puedo conseguir un plano del metro?
¿Dohn-deh pweh kohn-seh-geer oon plah-noh dehl meh-troh?

Where can I buy a metro ticket?
¿Dónde puedo comprar un billete de metro?
¿Dohn-deh pweh-doh kohm-prahr oon beel-yeh-teh deh meh-troh?

TRAVEL 15

Where can I get a taxi?	¿Dónde puedo tomar un taxi?	¿Dohn-deh pweh-doh tohm-mahr oon tahk-see?
I want to go to …	Quiero ir a…	Kee-ehr-oh eer ah…
How much will it cost to…. ?	¿Cuánto cuesta el billete para ir a… ?	¿Kwahn-toh kwehs-tah ehl beel-yeh-teh pah-rah eer ah… ?

… ON THE TRAIN

When is the next train for… ?	¿Cuándo sale el próximo tren para… ?	¿Kwahn-doh sah-leh ehl prohk-see-moh trehn pah-rah… ?
How often is the train for… ?	¿Con qué frecuencia salen los trenes para… ?	¿Kohn keh freh-kwen-thee-ah sah-lehn lohs trehn-ehs pah-rah… ?
Can I have a copy of the timetable?	¿Podría darme un horario, por favor?	¿Pohd-ree-ah dahr-meh oon ohr-ahr-ee-oh, pohr fah-vohr?
Where can I buy a ticket for… ?	¿Dónde puedo comprar un billete para ir a…?	¿Dohn-deh pweh-doh kohm-prahr oon beel-yeh-teh pah-rah eer ah…?

Two tickets for…	Dos billetes a…	Dohs beel-yeh-tehs ah…
Two single tickets for…	Dos billetes sencillos a…	Dohs beel-yeh-tehs sehn-theel-yohs ah
I'd like return tickets please.	Quiero billetes de ida y vuelta por favor.	Kee-ehr-oh beel-yet-tehs deh eed-ah ee bwehl-tah pohr fah-vohr.
I want to come back…	Quiero volver	Kee-ehr-oh bohl-behr
/today.	/hoy.	/oy.
/tomorrow.	/mañana.	/mah-nyahn-ah.
/in four days.	/cuatro días.	/kwa-tro dee-as.
Do I have to change?	¿Tengo que hacer transbordo?	¿Tehn-goh keh ah-thehr tranhs-bohr-doh?
Is there a fast train?	¿Hay un tren rápido?	¿I oon trehn rah-pee-doh?
What time does it arrive in… ?	¿A qué hora llega a… ?	¿Ah keh oh-rah yeh-gah a… ?
Which platform does the train for… leave from?	¿De qué andén sale el tren para… ?	¿Deh keh ahn-dehn sah-leh ehl trehn pah-rah…?
Is there a connection to… ?	¿Hay enlace a… ?	¿I ehn-lah-theh ah… ?

TRAVEL

... AT THE AIRPORT

English	Spanish	Pronunciation
Can I buy a ticket to... ?	Quiero un billete para...	Kee-ehr-oh oon beel-yeh-teh pah-rah...
Are there any supplements or taxes?	¿Hay que pagar suplementos o tasas?	¡I keh pah-gahr soo-pleh-mehn-tohs oh tah-sas?
I want an economy ticket.	Quiero un billete de clase turista.	Kee-ehr-oh oon beel-yeh-teh deh klah-seh too-rees-tah.
I want to fly business class.	Quiero volar en clase business.	Kee-ehr-oh boh-lahr ehn klah-seh bees-nehs.
Can I buy a ticket at the airport?	¿Puedo comprar un billete en el aeropuerto?	¿Pweh-doh kohm-prahr oon beel-yeh-teh ehn ehl ah-eh-roh-pwehr-toh?
How can I get to the airport?	¿Cómo puedo llegar al aeropuerto?	¿Kohm-oh pweh-doh yeh-gahr ahl ah-eh-roh-pwehr-toh?
What time must I check in?	¿A qué hora tengo que facturar el equipaje?	¿Ah keh oh-rah tehn-goh keh fahk-too-rahr ehl eh-kee-pah-khe?
Where is the check-in desk for flights to...?	¿Dónde está el mostrador de facturación para los vuelos a... ?	¿Dohn-deh ehs-tah ehl mohs-trah-dohr deh fahk-too-rah-thee-ohn pah-rah lohs bweh-lohs ah... ?
Can I check in, please?	Quiero facturar mi equipaje, por favor	Kee-ehr-oh fahk-too-rahr mee eh-kee-pah-kheh, pohr fah-vohr
Could I have an aisle seat?	¿Podría darme un asiento de pasillo?	¿Pohd-ree-ah dahr-meh oon ah-see-ehn-toh deh pah-seel-yo?
/window seat?	/de ventana?	/deh behn-tahn-ah?
Could I sit by the emergency exit?	¿Podría darme un asiento junto a la salida de emergencias?	¿Pohd-ree-ah dahr-meh oon ah-see-ehn-toh khoon-toh ah lah sah-lee-dah deh eh-mehr-khehn-thee-ahs?
Can I take this as hand luggage?	¿Puedo llevar esto de equipaje de mano?	¿Pweh-doh yeh-bahr ehs-toh deh eh-kee-pah-kheh deh mahn-noh?

TRAVEL 17

USEFUL WORDS

English	Spanish	Pronunciation
airport	**aeropuerto**	ah-eh-roh-pwehr-toh
arrivals	**llegadas**	yehg-ahd-ahs
bag	**bolsa**	bohl-sah
book	**libro**	leeb-roh
bus station	**estación de autobuses**	ehs-tah-thee-ohn deh ow-toh-boos-ehs
bus stop	**parada de autobús**	pahr-ah-dah deh ow-toh-boos
cancel	**cancelar**	kahn-theh-lahr
change	**cambiar**	kahm-bee-ahr
delay	**retraso**	reh-trah-soh
departures	**salidas**	sah-lee-dahs
early	**pronto**	prohn-toh
exit	**salida**	sah-lee-dah
hand luggage	**equipaje de mano**	eh-kee-pah-kheh deh mahn-noh
late	**tarde**	tahr-deh
luggage	**equipaje**	eh-kee-pah-kheh
map	**mapa**	mah-pah
passport	**pasaporte**	pah-sah-pohr-teh
place	**lugar**	loo-gahr
reserve	**reservar**	reh-seh-bahr
road	**carretera**	kah-rreht-ehr-ah
rucksack	**mochila**	moh-chee-lah
security check	**comprobación de seguridad**	kohm-proh-bah-thee-ohn deh seh-goo-ree-dahth
suitcase	**maleta**	mah-leh-tah
tax	**tasa**	tah-sah
taxi	**taxi**	tahk-see
ticket	**billete**	beel-yeh-teh
train station	**estación de trenes**	ehs-tah-thee-ohn deh trehn-ehs
underground	**metro**	meht-roh
visa	**visa**	bee-sah
walk	**andar**	ahn-dahr

RENTING A CAR

English	Spanish	Pronunciation
We have booked a rental car.	**Hemos reservado un coche de alquiler.**	Ehm-ohs reh-sehr-bah-doh oon koh-cheh deh ahl-keel-ehr.
👁 Could we rent a car please?	**Por favor, ¿podríamos alquilar un coche?**	Pohr fah-vohr, ¿pohd-ree-ah-mohs ahl-keel-ahr oon koh-cheh?
👁 How much is it for…	**¿Cuánto cuesta para…**	¿Kwahn-toh kwehs-tah pah-rah
/a week?	/**una semana?**	/oon-ah seh-mahn-ah?
/a day?	/**un día?**	/oon dee-ah?
Does the price include insurance?	**¿El precio incluye el seguro?**	¿Ehl preh-thee-oh een-kloo-yeh ehl seh-goo-roh?

18 TRAVEL

Is there anything else to pay?	¿Hay que pagar algo más?	¿I keh pah-gahr ahl-goh mahs?
Do I have to leave a deposit?	¿Tengo que dejar un depósito?	¿Tehn-goh keh deh-khahr oon deh-poh-see-toh?
Can I have...	¿Tienen un coche...	¿Tee-eh-nehn oon koh-cheh
/a cheaper car?	/más barato?	/mahs bah-rah-toh
/a bigger car?	/mas grande?	/mahs grahn-deh
Which number do we call if we break down?	¿Qué número debo marcar si tengo una avería?	¿Keh noo-mehr-oh deh-boh mahr-kahr see tehn-goh oon-ah ah-behr-ee-ah?
What sort of petrol does it take?	¿Qué tipo de combustible utiliza?	¿Keh tee-poh deh kohm-boos-teeb-leh oo-tee-lee-thah?
Where do we return the car?	¿Dónde tenemos que devolver el coche?	¿Dohn-deh ten-neh-mohs keh deh-bohl-behr ehl koh-cheh?
Can we leave the car at the airport?	¿Puedo devolver el coche en el aeropuerto?	¿Pweh-doh deh-bohl-behr ehl koh-cheh ehn ehl ah-eh-roh-pwehr-toh?
Where is the car?	¿Dónde está el coche?	¿Dohn-deh ehs-tah ehl koh-cheh?

HEARING

Can I see your licence?	¿Me podría enseñar su carné de conducir?	¿Meh pohd-ree-ah ehn-seh-nyahr soo kahr-neh deh kohn-doo-theer?
You must leave a deposit.	Tiene que pagar un depósito.	Tee-eh-neh keh pah-gahr oon deh-poh-see-toh.
How long do you want the car?	¿Para cuánto tiempo quiere el coche?	¿Pah-rah kwahn-toh tee-ehm-poh kee-ehr-eh ehl koh-cheh?

DRIVING

Is this the right road for...?	¿Es ésta la carretera que va a...?	¿Ehs ehs-tah lah kahrr-eh-tehr-rah keh bah ah...?
How do I get to the motorway?	¿Cómo puedo llegar a la autopista?	¿Koh-moh pweh-doh yeh-gahr ah lah ow-toh-pees-tah?
How far is it?	¿Está lejos?	¿Ehs-tah leh-khohs?

TRAVEL 19

Where is the nearest petrol station?	¿Dónde está la gasolinera más cercana?	¿Dohn-deh ehs-tah lah gah-soh-leen-nehr-ah mahs thehr-kahn-ah?
Full tank, please.	Lleno, por favor.	Yeh-noh, pohr fah-vohr.
I want to pay for the petrol on pump number....	Quiero pagar la gasolina del surtidor número…	Kee-ehr-oh pah-gahr lah gah-soh-leen-ah dehl soor-tee-dohr noo-mehr-oh…
Where are the air and water?	¿Dónde están el aire y el agua?	¿Dohn-deh ehs-tahn ehl ah-ee-reh ee ehl ah-gwah?
Where can I park?	¿Dónde puedo aparcar?	¿Dohn-deh pweh-doh ah-pahr-kahr?

PROBLEMS

Can you help me? I've broken down.	¿Puede ayudarme? Se me ha estropeado el coche.	¿Pweh-deh ah-yoo-dahr-meh? Seh meh ah ehs-troh-peh-ah-doh ehl koh-cheh.
Can you help me? I've run out of petrol.	¿Puede ayudarme? Me he quedado sin gasolina.	¿Pweh-deh ah-yoo-dahr-meh? Meh eh keh-dah-doh seen gah-soh-leen-nah.
I've had an accident.	He tenido un accidente.	Eh teh-nee-doh oon ahk-thee-dehn-teh.
My car has been stolen.	Me han robado el coche.	Meh ahn roh-bah-doh ehl koh-cheh.
Thanks for your help.	Gracias por su ayuda.	Grah-thee-ahs pohr soo ah-yoo-dah.

USEFUL WORDS

breakdown	avería	ah-behr-ee-ah
brakes	frenos	freh-nohs
car park	aparcamiento	ah-pahr-kah-myehnt-oh
clutch	embrague	ehm-brahg-eh
exhaust	tubo de escape	too-boh deh ehs-kah-peh
keys	llaves	yah-behs
licence	carné de conducir	karh-neh deh kohn-doo-theer
lock	cerradura	theh-rrah-door-ah
oil	aceite	ah-theh-ee-teh
overheating	sobrecalentamiento	soh-breh-kah-lehn-tah-myehn-toh
petrol	combustible	kohm-boos-teeb-leh
puncture	pinchazo	peen-chah-thoh
tyre	neumático	neh-oo-mah-tee-koh

TRAVEL

STAYING THE NIGHT

CHECKING IN

- I have a reservation. / Tengo una reserva. / Tehn-goh oon-ah reh-sehr-bah.
- Do you have a room for tonight? / ¿Tiene una habitación para esta noche? / ¿Tee-ehn-eh oon-ah ahb-ee-tah-thee-ohn pah-rah ehs-tah noh-cheh?
- I want a room for... / Quisiera una habitación para / Kee-see-ehr-ah oon-ah ahb-ee-tah-thee-ohn pah-rah
  - /one week. / /una semana. / /oon-ah seh-mahn-ah.
  - /one night. / /una noche. / /oon-ah noh-cheh
  - /three nights. / /tres noches. / /trehs noh-chehs
- How much is the room? / ¿Cuánto cuesta la habitación? / ¿Kwahn-toh kwehs-tah lah ahb-ee-tah-thee-ohn?
- Do you have a cheaper room? / ¿Tienen alguna habitación más barata? / ¿Tee-ehn-ehn ahl-goon-ah ahb-ee-tah-thee-ohn mahs bah-rah-tah?
- Does the price include breakfast? / ¿Está incluido el desayuno en el precio? / ¿Ehs-tah een-kloo-ee-doh ehl deh-sah-yoo-noh ehn ehl preh-thee-oh?
- Can I pay with a credit card? / ¿Puedo pagar con tarjeta de crédito? / ¿Pweh-doh pah-gahr kohn tahr-kheh-ta deh kreh-dee-toh?

CHECKING OUT

- What time must I check out? / ¿A qué hora tengo que dejar la habitación? / ¿Ah keh oh-rah tehn-goh keh deh-khahr lah ahb-ee-tah-thee-ohn?
- Can I pay the bill please? / Quiero pagar la cuenta por favor / Kee-ehr-oh pah-gahr lah kwehn-tah pohr fah-vohr

HOTELS AND GUESTHOUSES HEARING

- How many people? / ¿Cuántas personas son? / ¿Kwant-ahs pehr-sohn-ahs sohn?
- How long do you want to stay? / ¿Cuánto tiempo quiere quedarse? / ¿Kwahn-toh tee-ehm-poh kee-ehr-eh keh-dahr-seh?
- Do you have luggage? / ¿Lleva equipaje? / ¿Yeh-bah eh-kee-pah-kheh?
- Do you have a reservation? / ¿Tiene reserva? / ¿Tee-ehn-eh reh-sehr-bah?
- Sorry, we're full. / Lo lamento, estamos completos. / Loh lah-mehn-toh, ehs-tah-mohs kohm-pleh-tohs.
- No vacancies. / No hay habitaciones libres. / Noh I ahb-ee-tah-thee-ohn-ehs lee-brehs.

STAYING THE NIGHT – HOTELS AND GUESTHOUSES

ASKING FOR WHAT YOU WANT

English	Spanish	Pronunciation
I'd like...	Quiero...	Kee-ehr-oh...
/a single room.	/una habitación individual.	/oon-ah ahb-ee-tah-thee-ohn een-dee-bee-doo-ahl.
/a double room.	/una habitación doble.	/oon-ah ahb-ee-tah-thee-ohn doh-bleh.
I'd like a family room for two adults and...	Quiero una habitación familiar para dos adultos y	Kee-ehr-oh oon-ah ahb-ee-tah-thee-ohn fah-mee-lee-ahr pah-rah dohs ah-dool-tohs ee.
/two children.	/dos niños.	/dohs nee-nyohs.
/one child.	/un niño.	/oon neen-yoh.
I'd like a room with a bathroom.	Quiero una habitación con baño.	Kee-ehr-oh oon-ah ahb-ee-tah-thee-ohn kohn bah-nyoh.
I'd like a double bed.	Quiero una cama de matrimonio.	Kee-ehr-oh oon-ah kahm-ah deh mah-tree-moh-nee-oh.
I'd like twin beds.	Quiero dos camas.	Kee-ehr-oh dohs kahm-ahs.
Can I have a room with a view?	Quiero una habitación con vistas.	Kee-ehr-oh oon-ah ahb-ee-tah-thee-ohn kohn bees-tahs.
What time is breakfast?	¿A qué hora se sirve el desayuno?	¿Ah keh oh-rah seh seer-beh ehl deh-sah-yoo-noh?
What time is the front door locked?	¿A qué hora se cierra la puerta principal?	¿Ah keh oh-rah seh thee-ehrr-ah lah pwehr-tah preen-thee-pahl?
Will there be someone to let us in at ... o'clock?	¿Habrá alguien para dejarnos entrar a las...?	¿Ahb-rah ahlg-ee-ehn pah-rah deh-khahr-nohs ehn-trahr ah lahs...?
Is there a swimming pool here?	¿Hay piscina?	¿I pees-theen-nah?
Is there a restaurant in the hotel?	¿Hay restaurante en el hotel?	¿I rehs-tow-rahn-teh ehn ehl oh-tehl?
Can I have a cot for our baby?	¿Podría darnos una cuna para el bebé?	¿Pohd-ree-ah dahr-nohs oon-ah koon-ah pah-rah ehl beh-beh?
Can I leave this in the hotel safe?	¿Puedo dejar esto en la caja fuerte del hotel?	¿Pweh-doh deh-khahr ehs-toh ehn lah kah-hah fwehr-teh dehl oh-tehl?

22 STAYING THE NIGHT – HOTELS AND GUESTHOUSES

English	Spanish	Pronunciation
Where can I make a phone call?	¿Dónde puedo llamar por teléfono?	¿Dohn-deh pweh-doh yah-mahr pohr teh-leh-foh-noh?
Can I have breakfast in my room?	¿Podría desayunar en la habitación?	¿Pohd-ree-ah deh-sah-yoo-nahr ehn lah ahb-ee-tah-thee-ohn?
Can you wake me at … ?	¿Me podría despertar a las…?	¿Meh pohd-ree-ah dehs-pehr-tahr ah lahs…?
Can we leave our luggage?	¿Podemos dejar nuestro equipaje?	¿Poh-deh-mohs deh-khahr nwehs-troh eh-kee-pah-heh?
Are there any messages for me?	¿Hay algún mensaje para mí?	¿I ahl-goon mehn-sah-kheh pah-rah mee?

PROBLEMS

English	Spanish	Pronunciation
There's no hot water.	No hay agua caliente.	Noh I ah-gwah kahl-ee-ehn-te.
The light/the tv doesn't work.	La luz/la televisión no funciona.	Lah looth/lah teh-leh-bee-see-ohn noh foon-thee-ohn-ah.
I can't open the window.	No puedo abrir la ventana.	Noh pweh-doh ahb-reer lah behn-tahn-ah.
I've lost my key.	He perdido la llave.	Eh pehr-dee-doh lah yah-beh.
I'm locked out of my room.	Mi habitación está cerrada y no puedo entrar.	Mee ahb-ee-tah-thee-ohn ehs-tah thehrr-ah-dah ee noh pweh-doh ehn-trahr.
The door won't lock.	La puerta no se puede cerrar con llave.	Lah pwehr-tah noh seh pweh-deh thehr-rrahr kohn yah-beh.
Could we have	¿Podrían darme	¿Pohd-ree-ahn dar-meh
/clean towels	/toallas limpias?	/toh-ahl-yas leem-pee-ahs
/clean bedding	/sábanas limpias	/sahb-ah-nahs leem-pee-ahs
/another pillow?	/otra almohada?	/oh-trah ahl-moah-dah?
My room is too noisy.	En mi habitación hay demasiado ruido.	Ehn mee ahb-ee-tah-thee-ohn I deh-mah-see-ah-doh roo-ee-doh.
Can we have a different room?	¿Podría darnos otra habitación?	¿Pohd-ree-ah dahr-nohs oh-trah ahb-ee-tah-thee-ohn?
I think this bill is wrong – could you check it please?	Creo que hay un error en la factura – ¿podría revisarla, por favor?	Kreh-oh keh I oon eh-rrohr ehn lah fahk-toor-ah – ¿pohd-ree-ah reh-bee-sahr-lah, pohr fah-vohr?

STAYING THE NIGHT – HOTELS AND GUESTHOUSES

RENTING AND APARTMENTS

English	Spanish	Pronunciation
Where is the reception?	¿Dónde está la recepción?	¿Dohn-deh ehs-tah lah reh-thehp-thee-ohn?
Where can I collect the key?	¿Dónde puedo recoger la llave?	¿Dohn-deh pweh-doh reh-koh-khehr lah yah-beh?
Can I see the apartment?	¿Podría ver el apartamento?	¿Pohd-ree-ah behr ehl ah-pahr-tah-mehn-toh?
How much is the rent for…days?	¿Cuánto cuesta el alquiler para…días?	¿Kwahn-toh kwehs-tah ehl ahl-keel-ehr pah-rah…dee-ahs?
Where can I buy…	¿Dónde puedo comprar…	¿Dohn-deh pweh-doh kohm-prahr…
/milk?	/leche?	/leh-cheh?
/bread?	/pan?	/pahn?
Where does the rubbish go?	¿Dónde debo tirar la basura?	¿Dohn-deh deh-boh tee-rahr lah bah-soo-rah?
Can you show me how to work the…	¿Podría enseñarme cómo funciona…	¿Pohd-ree-ah ehn-seh-nyahr-meh koh-moh foon-thee-ohn-ah
/cooker?	/la cocina?	/lah koh-theen-ah?
/heating?	/la calefacción?	/lah kah-leh-fahk-thee-ohn?
/hot water?	/el agua caliente?	/ehl ah-gwah kahl-ee-ehn-teh?
/washing machine?	/la lavadora?	/lah lah-bah-dohr-ah?
Can we have some more bedding?	¿Podría darnos más ropa de cama?	¿Pohd-ree-ah dahr-nohs mahs roh-pah deh kah-mah?

USEFUL WORDS

English	Spanish	Pronunciation
apartment	apartamento	ah-pahr-tah-mehn-toh
balcony	balcón	bahl-kohn
bathroom	baño	bah-nyoh
bed and breakfast	alojamiento y desayuno	ah-loh-khah-myehn-toh ee deh-sah-yoo-noh
blanket	manta	mahn-tah
cooker	cocina	koh-theen-ah
corkscrew	sacacorchos	sah-kah-kohr-chohs
cutlery	cubiertos	koo-bee-ehr-tohs
day	día	dee-ah
dinner	cena	theh-nah
fridge	nevera	neh-behr-ah
full board	pensión completa	pehn-see-ohn kohm-pleh-tah

24 STAYING THE NIGHT – RENTING AND APARTMENTS

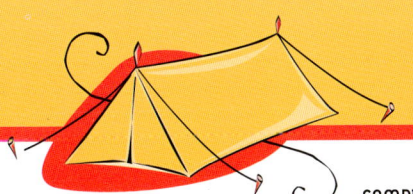

guesthouse	pensión	pehn-see-ohn
gym	gimnasio	kheem-nahs-ee-oh
half board	media pensión	meh-dee-ah pehn-see-ohn
hangers	perchas	pehr-chahs
hotel	hotel	oh-tehl
key	llave	yah-beh
lift	ascensor	ahs-thehn-sohr
light	luz	looth
lunch	almuerzo	ahl-mwehr-thoh
playground	parque	pahr-keh
plug	enchufe	ehn-choo-feh
reception	recepción	reh-thehp-thee-ohn
room	habitación	ah-bee-tah-thee-ohn
sauna	sauna	sahw-nah
shower	ducha	doo-chah
soap	jabón	khahb-ohn
swimming pool	piscina	pees-theen-ah
television	televisión	teh-leh-bee-see-ohn
tin opener	abrelatas	ahb-reh-lah-tahs
towel	toalla	toh-ahl-ya
week	semana	seh-mahn-ah

CAMPING AND CARAVANNING

- Where is the nearest campsite? — ¿Dónde está el camping más cercano? — ¿Dohn-deh ehs-tah ehl kahm-peeng mahs thehr-kah-noh?

I have booked a pitch. — He reservado una parcela. — Eh reh-sehr-bah-doh oon-ah pahr-theh-lah.

- Where do we go? — ¿Dónde tenemos que ir? — ¿Dohn-deh teh-neh-mohs keh eer?

- Can we put our... — ¿Podemos poner nuestra — ¿Poh-deh-mohs pohn-ehr nwehs-trah

  /caravan /tent ...here? — /caravana /tienda ...aquí? — /kah-rah-bahnah /tee-ehn-da ...ah-kee?

ASKING FOR WHAT YOU WANT

- Could we have a different pitch? — ¿Podría darnos otra parcela? — ¿Pohd-ree-ah dahr-nohs oh-trah pahr-theh-lah?

We'd like some shade. — Nos gustaría tener algo de sombra. — Nohs goos-tah-ree-ah tehn-ehr ahl-goh deh sohm-brah.

Are there any power points? — ¿Hay tomas eléctricas? — ¿I toh-mahs eh-lehk-tree-kahs?

STAYING THE NIGHT – CAMPING AND CARAVANNING

When...	¿Cuándo...	¿Kwahn-doh...
/does the shop open?	/abre la tienda?	/ahb-reh lah tee-ehn-dah?
/does the shop close?	/cierra la tienda?	/thee-ehrr-ah lah tee-ehn-dah?
Where is the drinking water?	¿Dónde está el agua potable?	¿Dohn-deh ehs-tah ehl ah-gwah poh-tahb-leh?
Is there a swimming pool on site?	¿Hay piscina en el camping?	¿I pees-theen-nah ehn ehl kahm-peeng?
Where are...	¿Dónde están...	¿Dohn-deh ehs-tahn...
/the showers?	/las duchas?	/lahs doo-chas?
/the toilets?	/los servicios?	/lohs sehr-bee-thee-ohs?
Is there somewhere I can...	¿Hay algún sitio donde pueda...	¿I ahl-goon see-tee-oh dohn-deh pweh-dah...
/dry clothes?	/secar la ropa?	/seh-kahr lah roh-pah?
/wash clothes?	/lavar la ropa?	/lah-bahr lah roh-pah?
Where can I get gas?	¿Dónde puedo comprar bombonas de gas?	¿Dohn-deh pweh-doh kohm-prahr bohm-boh-nahs deh gahs?

USEFUL WORDS

barbecue	barbacoa	bahr-bah-koh-ah
camp fire	hoguera	ohgh-ehr-ah
caravan	caravana	kah-rah-bahn-ah
cooker	cocina	koh-theen-ah
drinking water	agua potable	ah-gwah poh-tahb-leh
fire	fuego	fweh-goh
gas	gas	gahs
kitchen	cocina	koh-theen-ah
matches	cerillas	thehr-eel-yahs
pegs	pinzas	peen-thahs
rubbish	basura	bah-soo-rah
showers	duchas	doo-chahs
sleeping bag	saco de dormir	sah-koh deh dohr-meer
tent	tienda	tee-ehn-dah
washing line	cuerda de tender	kwehr-dah deh tehn-dehr

STAYING THE NIGHT – CAMPING AND CARAVANNING

LEISURE AND SPORT

LEISURE
ASKING FOR WHAT YOU WANT

How much does it cost to get in?	¿Cuánto cuesta la entrada?	¿Kwahn-toh kwehs-tah lah ehn-trah-dah?
...tickets, please.	...entradas, por favor?	...ehn-trah-dahs, pohr fah-vohr?
Is there a discount for...	¿Hay algún descuento para	¿I ahl-goon dehs-kwehn-toh pah-rah
/students?	/estudiantes?	/ehs-too-dee-ahn-tehs?
/children?	/niños?	/nee-nyos
Is there anything for the children to do?	¿Hay algún tipo de entretenimiento infantil?	¿I ahl-goon tee-poh deh ehn-treh-tehn-ee-myehn-toh een-fahn-teel?
Is there a guided tour?	¿Tienen visitas guiadas?	¿Tee-ehn-ehn bee-see-tahs ghee-ah-dahs?
Can we go inside?	¿Podemos entrar?	¿Poh-deh-mohs ehn-trahr?
Is it open all week?	¿Está abierto toda la semana?	¿Ehs-tah ahb-ee-ehr-toh toh-dah lah seh-mahn-ah?
Where is the tourist information?	¿Dónde está la oficina de turismo?	¿Dohn-deh ehs-tah lah oh-fee-theen-ah deh too-rees-moh?
Can you show me where I am?	¿Me podría indicar dónde estoy?	¿Meh pohd-ree-ah een-dee-kahr dohn-deh ehs-toy?
How can I get there?	¿Cómo puedo llegar hasta allí?	¿Koh-moh pweh-doh yeh-gahr ahs tah ah-yee?
What are the best things to see?	¿Cuáles son las principales atracciones turísticas?	¿Kwah-lehs sohn lahs preen-thee-pahl-ehs ah-trahk-thee-ohn-ehs too-rees-tee-kahs?
When are the markets?	¿Cuándo hay mercado?	¿Kwahn-doh I mehr-kah-doh?
Can I have a map of the city?	¿Me podría dar un plano de la ciudad?	¿Meh pohd-ree-ah dahr oon plah-noh deh lah thee-oo-dath?
I like ...	Me gusta...	Meh goos-tah...
/art.	/el arte.	/ehl ahr-teh.
/architecture.	/la arquitectura.	/lah ahr-kee-tehk-toor-ah.
/shopping.	/ir de compras.	/eer deh kohm-prahs.
/boat trips.	/los paseos en barca.	/lohs pah-seh-ohs ehn bahr-kah.
/history.	/la historia.	/lah ees-tor-ee-a.

HEARING

English	Spanish	Pronunciation
How many tickets do you want?	¿Cuántas entradas quiere?	¿Kwant-ahs ehn-trahd-dahs kee-ehr-eh?
The boat leaves at 3 o'clock.	El barco sale a las tres.	Ehl bahr-koh sah-leh ah lahs trehs.
We open at 10am.	Abrimos a las diez de la mañana.	Ahb-ree-mohs ah lahs dee-eth deh lah mah-nyah-nah.
We close at 6pm.	Cerramos a las seis de la tarde.	Theh-rrah-mohs ah lahs seh-ees deh lah tahr-deh.

USEFUL WORDS

English	Spanish	Pronunciation
admission	entrada	ehn-trah-dah
bridge	puente	pwehn-teh
castle	castillo	kahs-teel-yo
cathedral	catedral	kah-teh-drahl
cemetery	cementerio	theh-mehn-tehr-ee-oh
church	iglesia	eeg-leh-see-ah
closed	cerrado	theh-rrah-doh
ferry	ferry	feh-rree
gallery	galería	gah-lehr-ee-ah
guide	guía	ghee-ah
hotel	hotel	oh-tehl
museum	museo	moo-seh-oh
old town	casco antiguo	kahs-koh ahn-teeg-woh
opening hours	horario de apertura	oh-rah-ree-oh deh ah-pehr-toor-ah
palace	palacio	pah-lah-thee-oh
park	parque	pahr-keh
river	río	ree-oh
river trip	excursión por el río	ehks-koor-see-ohn pohr ehl ree-oh
shopping mall	centro comercial	thehn-troh kohm-ehr-thee-ahl
statue	estatua	ehs-tah-too-ah
tower	torre	toh-rreh
tour	tour	toor
zoo	zoo	thoh

SPORT

ASKING FOR WHAT YOU WANT

English	Spanish	Pronunciation
Where can we hire bicycles?	¿Dónde se pueden alquilar bicicletas?	¿Dohn-deh seh pweh-dehn ahl-keel-ahr bee-thee-kleh-tahs?
Where can we go walking?	¿Dónde se puede ir a dar un paseo?	¿Dohn-deh seh pweh-deh eer ah dahr oon pah-seh-oh?
Is there a path?	¿Hay camino?	¿I kah-meen-oh?
Is there a cycle path?	¿Hay carril para bicicletas?	¿I kah-rreel pah-rah bee-thee-kleh-tahs?

28 LEISURE AND SPORT

Where can we...	¿Dónde podemos...	¿Dohn-deh poh-deh-mohs...
/play tennis?	/jugar al tenis?	/khoo-gahr ahl teh-nees?
/play golf?	/jugar al golf?	/khoo-gahr ahl gohlf?
/play pool?	/jugar al billar?	/khoo-gahr ahl beel-yar?
/go ice skating?	/ir a patinar sobre hielo?	/eer ah pah-teen-ahr soh-breh iel-oh?
/go swimming?	/ir a nadar?	/eer ah nah-dahr?
⚽ Can I hire...	¿Puedo alquilar...	¿Pweh-doh ahl-keel-ahr...
/equipment?	/el equipo?	/ehl eh-keep-oh?
/a racket?	/una raqueta?	/oon-ah rah-keh-tah?
/clubs?	/palos?	/pah-lohs?
Where can we see...	¿Dónde podemos ver...	Dohn-deh poh-deh-mohs behr
/football?	/fútbol?	/foot-bohl?
/basketball?	/baloncesto?	bah-lohn-thehs-toh?
/horse racing?	/carreras de caballos?	/kah-rreh-rahs deh kah-bal-yohs?
⚽ Who's playing?	¿Quién juega?	¿Kee-ehn khweh-gah?
⚽ Where can we get tickets?	¿Dónde se pueden comprar las entradas?	¿Dohn-deh seh pweh-dehn kohm-prahr lahs ehn-trah-dahs?

USEFUL WORDS

bait	cebo	theh-boh
club	club	kloob
fishing	pesca	pehs-kah
fly	volar	boh-lahr
football	fútbol	foot-bohl
golf	golf	gohlf
gym	gimnasio	kheem-nahs-ee-oh
join	apuntarse	ah-poon-tahr-seh
point	punto	poon-toh
racket	raqueta	rah-keh-tah
rod	caña de pescar	kah-nyah deh pehs-kahr
score	puntuación	poon-too-ah-thee-ohn
sauna	sauna	sahw-nah
swimming pool	piscina	pees-theen-nah
tennis	tenis	teh-nees

LEISURE AND SPORT

EATING OUT

SNACKS, CAFÉS AND BARS

English	Spanish	Pronunciation
Excuse me. Waiter!	Disculpe. ¡Camarero!	Dees-kool-peh. ¡Kah-mahr-ehr-oh!
I'd like... /a beer.	Quiero... /una cerveza.	Kee-ehr-oh... /oon-ah thehr-beh-thah.
/a coffee.	/un café.	/oon kah-feh.
/a coffee with milk.	/un café con leche.	/oon kah-feh kohn leh-cheh.
/a tea with milk.	/un té con leche.	/oon teh kohn leh-cheh.
/an orange juice.	/un zumo de naranja.	/oon thoo-moh deh nah-rahn-khah.
/a mineral water.	/un agua mineral.	/oon ah-gwah meen-ehr-ahl.
Can I sit here?	¿Puedo sentarme aquí?	¿Pweh-doh sehn-tahr-meh ah-kee?
What soft drinks do you have?	¿Qué refrescos tiene?	¿Keh reh-frehs-kohs tee-ehn-eh?
Another drink please.	Quiero otra bebida, por favor.	Kee-ehr-oh oh-trah beh-bee-dah, pohr fah-vohr.
The same again.	Otro/a, por favor.	Oh-troh/trah, pohr fah-vohr.
What snacks do you have?	¿Qué tiene de picar?	¿Keh tee-ehn-eh deh pee-kahr?
Do you sell cigarettes?	¿Venden tabaco?	¿Behn-dehn tah-bahk-oh?
Where are the toilets?	¿Dónde están los servicios?	¿Dohn-deh ehs-tahn lohs sehr-bee-thee-ohs?
Can I have the bill please?	La cuenta, por favor	Lah kwehn-tah, pohr fah-vohr.

HEARING AND READING

English	Spanish	Pronunciation
What can I get you?	¿En qué puedo ayudarle?	¿Ehn keh pweh-doh ah-yoo-dahr-leh?
What would you like?	¿Qué desea?	¿Keh deh-seh-ah?
Would you like anything else?	¿Quiere algo más?	¿Kee-ehr-eh ahl-goh mahs?
What would you like to...	¿Qué quiere...	¿Keh kee-ehr-eh...
/drink?	/beber?	/beh-behr?
/eat?	/comer?	/kohm-ehr?
The specials are on the board.	Las sugerencias del chef están en la pizarra.	Lahs soo-khehr-ehn-thee-ahs dehl chehf ehs-tahn ehn la pee-thah-rrah
Service (not) included	El servicio (no) está incluido.	Ehl sehr-bee-thee-oh (no) ehs-tah een-kloo-ee-doh.

USEFUL WORDS

a lot	mucho	moo-choh
a little	poco	poh-koh
beer	cerveza	thehr-beh-thah
bill	cuenta	kwehn-tah
bottle of /half	botella de/media	boh-tehl-yah de/meh-dee-ah
brandy	brandy	brahn-dee
breakfast	desayuno	deh-sah-yoo-noh
cider	sidra	see-drah
cocktail	cóctel	kohk-tehl
gin	ginebra	khee-neh-brah
inside	dentro	dehn-troh
lager	cerveza rubia	thehr-beh-thah roo-bee-ah
lunch	almuerzo	ahl-mwerth-oh
one litre /half litre	un litro /medio litro	oon lee-troh /meh-dee-oh lee-tro
menu	carta	kahr-tah
outside	fuera	fwehr-ah
peanuts	cacahuetes	kah-kah-weh-tehs
port	oporto	oh-pohr-to
rum	ron	rohn
snack	algo de picar	ahl-goh deh pee-kahr
sparkling	con gas	kohn gahs
table	mesa	meh-sah
tap water	agua del grifo	ah-gwah dehl gree-foh
whiskey	whisky	wees-kee
wine	vino	been-oh

RESTAURANTS

Do you have a table?	¿Tienen una mesa libre?	¿Tee-ehn-ehn oon-ah meh-sah lee-breh?
Can we sit here?	¿Podemos sentarnos aquí?	¿Poh-deh-mohs sehn-tahr-nohs ah-kee?
A table for two/four please.	Una mesa para dos/cuatro, por favor.	Oon-ah meh-sah pah-rah dohs/kwah-troh, pohr fah-vohr.
Do you take credit cards?	¿Puedo pagar con tarjeta de crédito?	¿Pweh-doh pah-gahr kohn tahr-kheh-ta deh kreh-dee-toh?
Can we reserve a table for...	¿Queremos reservar una mesa para...	¿Keh-reh-mohs reh-sehr-bahr oon-ah meh-sah pah-rah...
/later?	/más tarde?	/mahs tahr-deh?
/this evening?	/esta noche?	/eh-stah noh-cheh?
/tomorrow?	/mañana?	/mah-nyah-nah?

EATING OUT – RESTAURANTS

English	Spanish	Pronunciation
The menu, please.	La carta, por favor.	Lah kahr-tah, pohr fah-vohr.
What are the specials?	¿Cuáles son las sugerencias del día?	¿Kwahl-ehs sohn lahs soo-khehr-ehn-thee-ahs dehl dee-ah?
I'd like the special.	Quiero la sugerencia del chef.	Kee-ehr-oh lah soo-khehr-ehn-thee-ah dehl chehf.
What's in this?	¿De qué está hecho esto?	¿Deh keh ehs-tah eh-choh ehs-toh?
How is this cooked?	¿Cómo está preparado esto?	¿Koh-moh ehs-tah preh-pah-rah-doh ehs-toh?
Is this	¿Es un plato	¿Ehs oon plah-toh
/hot?	/caliente	/kah-lee-ehn-teh
/spicy?	/picante?	/pee-kahn-teh?
Does this come with...	¿Este plato lleva...	¿Ehs-teh plah-toh yeh-bah...
/vegetables?	/verduras?	/behr-doo-rahs?
/salad?	/ensalada?	/ehn-sah-lah-dah?
/chips?	/patatas fritas?	/pah-tah-tahs free-tahs?
/sauce?	/salsa?	/sahl-sah?
Is service included?	¿El servicio está incluido?	¿Ehl sehr-bee-thee-oh ehs-tah een-kloo-ee-doh?
That was very good.	Estaba muy bueno.	Ehs-tah-bah mwee bweh-noh.

HEARING

English	Spanish	Pronunciation
Can I take your coat?	¿Me da su abrigo, por favor?	¿Meh dah soo ahb-ree-goh, pohr fah-vohr?
What would you like to drink?	¿Qué quieren de beber?	¿Keh kee-ehr-ehn deh beh-behr?
What can I get you?	¿Qué desean?	¿Keh deh-seh-ahn?

PROBLEMS

How much longer will the food be?	¿Cuánto va a tardar la comida?	¿Kwahn-toh bah ah tahr-dahr lah kohm-ee-dah?
Could you get us a drink while we're waiting?	¿Podría traernos algo de beber mientras esperamos?	¿Pohd-ree-ah trah-ehr-nohs ahl-goh deh beh-behr myehn-trahs ehs-peh-rah-mohs?
Could we have some bread while we're waiting?	¿Podría traernos pan mientras esperamos?	¿Pohd-ree-ah trah-ehr-nohs pahn myehn-trahs ehs-peh-rah-mohs?
This isn't what I ordered.	Esto no es lo que he pedido.	Ehs-toh noh ehs loh keh eh peh-dee-doh.

This tastes odd.	**Esto sabe raro.**	Ehs-toh sah-beh rahr-oh.
My food is cold.	**La comida está fría.**	Lah kohm-ee-dah ehs-tah free-ah.
I don't have my wallet.	**No llevo la cartera.**	Noh yeh-boh lah kahr-tehr-ah.
I don't have enough money with me.	**No llevo suficiente dinero.**	Noh yeh-boh soo-fee-thee-ehnt-teh deen-ehr-oh.

READING THE MENU

anchovies	**anchoas**	ahn-choh-ahs
artichoke	**alcachofas**	ahl-kah-choh-fahs
bacon	**bacon**	beh-kohn
baked	**cocido**	koh-thee-doh
beef	**ternera**	tehr-nehr-ah
beans	**judías**	khoo-dee-ahs
boiled	**hervido**	ehr-bee-doh
bread	**pan**	pahn
braised	**cocido a fuego lento**	koh-thee-doh ah fweh-goh lehn-toh
butter	**mantequilla**	mahn-tehk-eel-ya
cabbage	**col**	kohl
carrots	**zanahorias**	thah-nah-ohr-ee-ahs
cheese	**queso**	keh-soh
– goats' cheese	**– de cabra**	– deh kahb-rah
– blue cheese	**– azul**	– ah-thool
chicken	**pollo**	pohl-yoh
chips	**patatas fritas**	pah-tah-tahs free-tahs
chops	**chuletas**	choo-leh-tahs
cold	**frío**	free-oh
course	**plato**	plah-toh
crab	**cangrejo**	kahn-grekh-hoh
cream	**nata**	nah-tah
duck	**pato**	pah-toh
dumplings	**albóndigas de pasta**	ahl-bohn-dee-gahs deh pahs-tah
eggs	**huevos**	weh-bohs
fish	**pescado**	pehs-kah-doh
flan	**flan**	flahn
fried	**frito**	free-toh
garlic	**ajo**	ah-khoh
goose	**oca**	oh-kah
gravy	**salsa**	sahl-sah
green beans	**judías verdes**	khoo-dee-ahs behr-dehs
ham	**jamón**	khah-mohn
heart	**corazón**	koh-rah-thohn
honey	**miel**	myehl
horse	**caballo**	kah-bahl-yoh
hot	**caliente**	kahl-ee-ehn-teh
jam	**mermelada**	mehr-mehl-ah-dah
kidney	**riñón**	ree-nyohn

EATING OUT – READING THE MENU   33

English	Spanish	Pronunciation
lamb	cordero	korh-dehr-oh
leek	puerro	pweh-rroh
lentils	lentejas	lehn-teh-khas
liver	higado	ee-gah-doh
lobster	langosta	lahng-ohst-ah
loin	lomo	lohm-oh
main course	plato principal	plah-toh preen-thee-pahl
marinated	marinado	mahr-een-ah-doh
mussels	mejillones	meh-kheel-yohn-ehs
mutton	cordero	korh-dehr-oh
olive oil	aceite de oliva	ah-theh-ee-teh deh oh-leeb-ah
oysters	ostras	ohs-trahs
pancakes	crepes	krehps
paté	paté	pah-teh
pasta	pasta	pahs-tah
pastry	hojaldre	oh-khahl-dreh
peas	guisantes	ghee-sahn-tehs
pie	tarta	tahr-tah
poached	escalfado	ehs-kahl-fah-doh
pork	cerdo	thehr-doh
potatoes	patatas	pah-tah-tahs
- mashed	- puré	- poo-reh
- fried	- fritas	- free-tahs
- chipped	- troceadas	- trohtheh-ah-dohs
- boiled	- hervidas	- ehr-bee-dahs
- roast	- asadas	- ah-sah-dahs
pudding	pudding	poo-deen
rabbit	conejo	kohn-eh-kho
red beans	judías pintas	khoo-dee-ahs peen-tahs
rice	arroz	ah-rroth
roast	asado	ah-sah-do
rolls	rollo	rohl-yo
salad	ensalada	ehn-sah-lah-dah
sauce	salsa	sahl-sah
sausage	salchicha	sahl-chee-chah
sea food	marisco	mahr-ees-koh
snails	caracoles	kah-rah-koh-lehs
soup	sopa	soh-pah
spicy	picante	pee-kahn-teh
starter	entrante	ehn-trahn-teh
steak	filete	feel-eh-teh
stewed	estofado	ehs-toh-fah-doh
toast	tostada	tohs-tah-dah
tomatoes	tomates	tohm-ah-tehs
tripe	callos	kahl-yohs
trout	trucha	trooch-ah
tuna	atún	ah-toon
veal	ternera	tehr-nehr-ah
vegetables	verduras	behr-doo-rahs
water (still /sparkling)	agua (sin gas /con gas)	ah-gwah (seen gahs/ kohn gahs)
wine	vino	been-oh
- white	- blanco	- blahn-koh
- red	- tinto	- teen-toh
- table	- de mesa	- deh meh-sah

EATING OUT – READING THE MENU

BUSINESS

INTRODUCTIONS & GREETINGS

How are you?	¿Cómo está usted?	¿Koh-moh ehs-tah oos-teth?
😊 Delighted to meet you.	Encantado de conocerle.	Ehn-kahn-tah-doh deh koh-oh-thehr-leh.
😊 Nice to see you again.	Encantado de volver a verle.	Ehn-kahn-tah-doh deh bohl-behr ah behr-leh.
Let me introduce my colleague.	Le presento a mi colega.	Leh preh-sehn-toh ah mee koh-leh-gah.
This is...	Éste/a es...	Ehs-teh/tah ehs...

ASKING FOR WHAT YOU WANT

Can you show me...	¿Podría enseñarme...	¿Pohd-ree-ah ehn-seh-nyahr-meh...
/designs?	/los diseños?	/lohs dee-seh-nyohs?
/pictures?	/las fotos?	/lahs foh-tohs?
/figures?	/las cifras?	/lahs thee-frahs?
/projections?	/las proyecciones?	/lahs proh-yehk-thee-ohn-ehs?
/the new line?	/la nueva línea?	/lah nweh-bah leen-yah?
😊 When will these be ready?	¿Cuándo estarán listos?	¿Kwahn-doh ehs-tah-rahn lees-os?

😊 Could you repeat that?	¿Podría repetirlo, por favor?	¿Pohd-ree-ah reh-peh-teer-loh, pohr fah-vohr?
I'd like to check...	Me gustaría comprobar...	Meh goos-tah-ree-ah kohm-proh-bahr...
/the sizes.	/las tallas.	/lahs tahl-yahs.
/the colours.	/los colores.	/lohs koh-lohr-ehs.
I'd like to make an order for...	Quiero hacer un pedido de...	Kee-ehr-oh ah-thehr oon peh-dee-doh de...
Would you send me...?	¿Podría enviarme...?	¿Pohd-ree-ah ehn-bee-ahr-meh...?
We need...	Necesitamos...	Neh-theh-see-tah-mohs...
/more time.	/más tiempo.	/mahs tee-ehm-poh.
/more information.	/más información.	/mahs een-fohr-mahth-ee-ohn.
/a better idea of what you need.	/tener una idea más clara de sus necesidades.	/teh-nehr oon-ah ee-deh-ah mahs klah-rah deh soos neh-theh-see-dah-dehs.

BUSINESS 35

INFORMATION AND DISCUSSING BUSINESS

English	Spanish	Pronunciation
We have different... /sizes /colours.	**Tenemos varias... /tallas /colores.**	Teh-neh-mohs bah-ree-ahs... /tahl-yahs /koh-loh-rehs.
Would you like to see some samples?	**¿Quiere ver unas muestras?**	¿Kee-ehr-eh behr oon-ahs mwehs-trahs?
I can leave these with you.	**Puedo dejárselo para que lo vea.**	Pweh-doh deh-khahr-seh-loh pah-rah keh loh beh-ah.
I will check the delivery dates for you.	**Comprobaré las fechas de entrega.**	Kohm-proh-bahr-eh lahs feh-chahs deh ehn-treh-gah.
Thank you for your order.	**Gracias por el pedido.**	Grah-thee-ahs pohr ehl peh-dee-doh.
I can come back to you with a price later.	**Más adelante podría darle un precio.**	Mahs ah-deh-lahn-teh pohd-ree-ah dahr-leh oon preh-thee-oh.
This is our best price.	**Éste es nuestro mejor precio.**	Ehs-teh ehs nwehs-troh meh-khohr preh-thee-oh.
This price is in Euros.	**Este precio está en euros.**	Ehs-teh preh-thee-oh ehs-tah ehn eh-oo-rohs.
We need payment before sending the goods.	**Necesitamos que efectúe el pago antes de que enviemos los productos.**	Neh-theh-see-tah-mohs keh eh-fehk-too-eh ehl pah-goh ahn-tehs deh keh ehn-bee-eh-mohs lohs proh-dook-tohs.
We can offer you credit terms.	**Podemos darle facilidades de crédito.**	Poh-deh-mohs dahr-leh fah-thee-lee-dah-dehs deh kreh-dee-toh.
We can send... /these /it /straight away.	**Podemos /mandarlos /mandarlo /ahora mismo.**	Poh-deh-mohs /mahn-dahr-los /mahn-dahr-loh /ah-ohr-ah mees-moh.
/next week.	**/la semana que viene.**	/lah seh-mahn-ah keh bee-ehn-neh.
/next month.	**/el mes que viene.**	/ehl mehs keh bee-ehn-neh.
I need to check that with...	**Esto tengo que preguntárselo...**	Ehs-toh tehn-goh keh preh-goon-tarse-lo...
/my colleagues.	**/a mis compañeros.**	/ah mees kom-pah-nyeh-rohs.
/with head office.	**/a la central.**	/ah lah thehn-trahl.

36 BUSINESS

Shall we talk about…	¿Hablamos de…	¿Ahb-lah-mohs deh…
/prices?	/los precios?	/lohs preh-thee-ohs?
/terms?	/las condiciones?	/lahs kohn-dee-thee-ohn-ehs?
/credit?	/el crédito?	/ehl kreh-dee-toh?
/delivery dates?	/las fechas de entrega?	/lahs feh-chahs deh ehn-treh-gah?
Can we talk about…?	¿Podemos hablar sobre…?	¿Poh-deh-mohs ahb-lahr sohb-reh…?
/the brief?	/el orden del día?	/ehl ohr-dehn dehl dee-ah?
/your needs?	/sus necesidades?	/soos ne-theh-see-dah-dehs?
/the audience?	/el tipo de cliente?	ehl tee-poh deh klee-ehn-teh?
/the targets?	/los objetivos?	/lohs ohb-kleh-tee-bohs?
/alternatives?	/las alternativas?	/lahs ahl-tehr-nah-tee-bahs?
/the competition?	/la competencia?	/lah kohm-peh-tehn-thee-ah?
I would like some information about…	Me gustaría tener información sobre…	Meh goos-tah-ree-ah teh-nehr een-fohr-mah-thee-ohn sohb-reh…

AGREEING AND DISAGREEING

That's a good idea.	Me parece una buena idea.	Meh pah-reh-theh oon-ah bweh-nah ee-deh-ah.
That's an excellent idea.	Me parece una idea excelente.	Meh pah-reh-theh oon-ah ee-deh-ah ehk-thehl-ehn-teh.
I like this/it very much. It's not bad.	Me gusta mucho/esto. No está mal.	Meh goos-tah moo-choh/ehs-toh. Noh ehs-tah mahl.
I don't like this.	No me gusta nada esto.	Noh me goos-tah nah-dah ehs-toh.
I don't like it at all. It's nothing special.	No me gusta nada. No es nada especial.	Noh me goos-tah nah-dah. Noh ehs nah-dah ehs-peh-thee-ahl.
It's not possible.	No es posible.	Noh ehs poh-see-bleh.
I agree entirely.	Estoy completamente de acuerdo.	Ehs-toy kohm-pleh-tah-mehn-teh deh ah-kwehr-doh.
I really don't agree.	La verdad es que no estoy de acuerdo.	Lah behr-dath ehs keh noh ehs-toy deh ah-kwehr-doh.

BUSINESS 37

🔊 Shall we meet again later?	¿Quedamos otra vez más tarde?	¿Keh-dah-mohs oh-trah beth mahs tahr-deh?
Ok, see you later.	Vale, hasta luego.	Bah-leh, ahs-tah lweh-goh.
What about tomorrow?	¿Qué le parece mañana?	¿Keh leh pah-reh-theh mah-nyah-nah?
I have another meeting...	Tengo otra reunión...	Tehn-goh oh-trah reh-oo-nee-ohn...
/in half an hour	/dentro de media hora.	/dehn-troh deh meh-dee-ah oh-rah.
/tomorrow.	/mañana.	/mah-nyah-nah
/after this one.	/después de ésta.	/dehs-pwehs deh ehs-tah.

USEFUL WORDS

agreement	contrato	kohn-trah-toh
brief	orden del día	ohr-dehn dehl dee-ah
busy	ocupado	oh-koo-pah-doh
buying	comprar	kohm-prahr
colour	color	koh-lohr
competitor	competencia	kohm-peh-tehn-thee-ah
credit	crédito	kreh-dee-toh
customer	cliente	klee-ehn-teh
customs	aduanas	ahd-wahn-ahs
deadline	fecha límite	feh-chah lee-mee-teh
delivery	entrega	ehn-treh-gah
design	diseño	dee-seh-nyoh
idea	idea	ee-deh-ah
market	mercado	mehr-kah-doh
material	material	mah-tehr-ee-ahl
meeting	reunión	reh-oo-nee-ohn
product	producto	proh-dook-toh
quality	calidad	kah-lee-dath
report	informe	een-fohr-meh
sale	venta	behn-tah
samples	muestras	mwehs-trahs
size	talla	tahl-yah
terms	condiciones	kohn-dee-thee-ohn-ehs
trade	comercio	kohm-ehr-thee-oh
unique	único	oon-ee-koh
unit	unidad	oon-ee-dath
warehouse	almacén	ahl-mah-thehn
weight	peso	peh-soh
work	trabajo	trah-bah-khoh

38 BUSINESS

SHOPPING

HEARING

Can I help you?	¿Puedo ayudarle?	¿Pweh-doh ah-yoo-dahr-leh?
Would you like anything else?	¿Desea algo más?	¿Deh-seh-ah ahl-goh mahs?
We don't accept this card here.	No aceptamos esta tarjeta.	Noh ath-ehp-tah-mohs ehs-tah tahr-kheh-ta.
Can I get you a different size?	¿Quiere que le traiga otra talla?	¿Kee-ehr-eh keh leh trah-ee-gah oh-trah tahl-yah?

PAYING AND PRICES

Can I use this card here?	¿Puedo pagar con esta tarjeta?	¿Pweh-doh pah-gahr kohn ehs-tah tahr-kheh-ta?
Can I pay please?	Quisiera pagar, por favor	Kee-see-ehr-ah pah-gahr, pohr fah-vohr
How much is this?	¿Cuánto cuesta esto?	¿Kwahn-toh kwehs-tah ehs-toh?

FOOD AND BASICS

Do you have...?	¿Tiene...?	¿Tee-ehn-eh...?
Can I have...	Quiero...	Kee-ehr-oh...
/that piece?	/ese trozo?	/eh-seh troh-thoh
/100 grams	/cien gramos.	/thee-ehn grah-mohs
/250 grams	/dos cientos cinchenta gramos	/dohs thee-ehn-tohs theen-kwehn-tah grah-mohs
...of ham?	...de jamón.	...deh khah-mohn.
/half a kilo of this cheese?	/medio kilo de este queso?	/meh-dee-oh kee-loh deh ehs-teh keh-soh?
/one piece?	/un trozo?	/oon troh-thoh?
/two pieces?	/dos trozos?	/dohs troh-thohs?
/a bit more?	/un poco más?	/oon poh-koh mahs?
/a bit less?	/un poco menos?	/oon poh-koh meh-nohs?
/half a kilo?	/medio kilo?	/meh-dee-oh kee-loh?
/one kilo?	/un kilo?	/oon kee-loh?
/500 grams of...	/quinientos gramos de...	/kee-nee-ehn-tohs grah-mohs deh...
/that.	/eso.	/eh-soh.
/the meat.	/carne.	/kahr-neh.
/the sausage.	/salchicha.	/sahl-chee-chah.
/the cheese.	/queso.	/keh-soh.
/the fish.	/pescado.	/pehs-kah-doh.
How much is...?	¿Cuánto cuesta...?	¿Kwahn-toh kwehs-tah...?
May I taste a piece of this please?	¿Podría probar un trocito de esto, por favor?	¿Pohd-ree-ah proh-bahr oon troh-thee-toh deh ehs-toh, pohr fah-vohr?
Is this food spicy?	¿Esta comida es picante?	¿Ehs-tah kohm-ee-dah ehs pee-kahn-teh?

SHOPPING 39

Is this sweet?	¿Es dulce?	¿Ehs dool-theh?
How long will this keep?	¿Cuánto tiempo se puede guardar?	¿Kwahn-toh tee-ehm-poh seh pweh-deh gwahr-dahr?

USEFUL WORDS

apples	manzanas	mahn-thah-nahs
baby food	comida para bebés	kohm-ee-dah pah-rah beh-behs
baby milk	leche para bebés	leh-cheh pah-rah beh-behs
batteries	pilas	pee-lahs
candles	velas	beh-lahs
cheese	queso	keh-soh
coffee	café	kah-feh
fresh	fresco	frehs-koh
frozen	congelado	kohn-kheh-lah-doh
fruit	fruta	froo-tah
gas	gas	gahs
joint of (meat)	corte de	kohr-teh deh
lemon	limón	lee-mohn
matches	cerillas	thehr-eel-yahs
melons	melones	meh-loh-nehs
milk	leche	leh-cheh
- fresh milk	- leche fresca	-leh-cheh frehs-kah
- long life	- uperizada	- oop-ehr-ee-thah-dah
mushrooms	champiñones	chahm-pee-nyoh-nehs
nappies	pañales	pah-nyah-lehs
oil	aceite	ah-theh-ee-teh
olives	aceitunas	ah-theh-ee-too-nahs
onions	cebollas	theh-bol-yahs
orange	naranja	nah-rahn-khah
peaches	melocotones	meh-loh-koh-toh-nehs
pepper	pimienta	pee-mee-ehn-tah
salt	sal	sahl
soap	jabón	khah-bohn
stock	caldo	kahl-doh
shellfish	marisco	mahr-ees-koh
tin opener	abrelatas	ahb-reh-lah-tahs
toilet paper	papel higiénico	pah-pehl ee-khee-ehn-ee-koh
toothpaste	pasta de dientes	pahs-tah deh dyehn-tehs
washing powder	detergente para la ropa	deh-tehr-khehn-teh pah-rah lah roh-pah
washing-up liquid	detergente para la vajilla	deh-tehr-khehn-teh pah-rah lah bah-kheel-yah
water	agua	ah-gwah
wine	vino	been-oh

SHOPPING

SHOPS AND SERVICES

Where is the nearest…?	¿Dónde está el/la…más cercano/a?	¿Dohn-deh ehs-tah ehl/lah… mahs thehr-kahn-oh/ah?
Can you repair this?	¿Pueden arreglar esto?	¿Pweh-dehn ah-rreh-glahr ehs-toh?
How long will it take?	¿Cuánto tardará?	¿Kwahn-toh tahr-dahr-ah?
I'd like this film developed.	Quiero revelar este carrete.	Kee-ehr-oh reh-beh-lahr ehs-teh kah-rreh-teh.
How much will it cost?	¿Cuánto va a costar?	¿Kwahn-toh bah ah kohs-tahr?
Can I have this cleaned?	¿Podrían limpiar esto?	¿Pohd-ree-ahn leem-pee-ahr ehs-toh?
When can I collect it?	¿Cuándo puedo recogerlo?	¿Kwahn-doh pweh-doh reh-koh-khehr-loh?
When do you… /open? /close?	¿Cuándo… /abren? /cierran?	¿Kwahn-doh… /ah-rehn? /thee-eh-rrahn?

PROBLEMS

This doesn't work.	Esto no funciona	Ehs-toh noh foon-thee-ohn-ah
This doesn't fit.	Esto no queda bien.	Ehs-toh noh keh-dah bee-ehn.
You've charged me too much.	Me ha cobrado demasiado.	Meh ah koh-brah-doh deh-mah-see-ah-doh.
You haven't given me enough change.	No me ha devuelto bien el cambio.	Noh meh ah deh-bwehl-toh bee-ehn ehl kahm-bee-oh.
I'd like a refund.	Quisiera devolverlo.	Kee-see-ehr-ah deh-bohl-behr-loh.
I wasn't given a receipt.	No me han dado el ticket.	Noh meh ahn dah-doh ehl tee-keht.
Please can I see the manager.	¿Podría hablar con el encargado, por favor?	¿Pohd-ree-ah ahb-lahr kohn ehl ehn-kahr-gah-doh, pohr fah-vohr?

SHOPPING – SHOPS AND SERVICES

USEFUL WORDS – SHOPPING

bakery	**horno**	ohr-noh
book shop	**librería**	lee-breh-ree-ah
butcher	**carnicería**	kahr-nee-theh-ree-ah
camera shop	**tienda de fotografía**	tee-ehn-da deh foh-toh-grah-fee-ah
chemist	**farmacia**	fahr-mah-thee-ah
clothes shop	**tienda de ropa**	tee-ehn-da deh roh-pah
deli	**charcutería**	chahr-koh-teh-ree-ah
fishmonger	**pescadería**	pehs-kahd-ehr-ee-ah
greengrocer	**verdulería**	behr-dool-ehr-ee-ah
hardware store	**ferretería**	fehr-reht-eh-ree-ah
jewellers	**joyería**	khoy-ehr-ee-ah
map	**plano**	plah-noh
market	**mercado**	mehr-kah-doh
music shop	**tienda de música**	tee-ehn-da deh moo-see-kah
off licence	**tienda de licores**	tee-ehn-da deh lee-kohr-ehs
shoe shop	**zapatería**	thah-paht-ehr-ee-ah
shoe repair shop	**zapatero**	thah-paht-ehr-oh
supermarket	**supermercado**	soo-pehr-mehr-kah-doh
tobacconist	**estanco**	ehs-tahn-koh
toy shop	**juguetería**	khoo-ghet-ehr-ee-ah

USEFUL WORDS – SERVICES

car hire	**alquiler de coches**	ahl-keel-ehr deh koh-chehs
dentist	**dentista**	dehn-tees-tah
doctor	**médico**	meh-dee-koh
dry cleaners	**tintorería**	teen-tohr-ehr-ee-ah
garage	**taller**	tahl-yehr
hairdresser	**peluquería**	pehl-ook-ehr-ee-ah
police station	**comisaría**	kohm-ees-ahr-ee-ah
post office	**correos**	ko-rreh-ohs
travel agent	**agencia de viajes**	ah-khehn-thee-ah deh bee-ah-khehs

SHOPPING – SHOPS AND SERVICES

CLOTHES AND GIFTS

🎧 Where is the main shopping street?	¿Dónde está la principal calle comercial?	¿Dohn-deh ehs-tah lah preen-thee-pal kahl-yeh kohm-ehr-thee-ahl?
Is it far from here?	¿Está lejos de aquí?	¿Ehs-tah leh-khohs deh ah-kee?
Can I walk?	¿Se puede ir andando?	¿Seh pweh-deh eer ahn-dahn-doh?
🎧 What size is this?	¿Qué talla es esto?	¿Keh tahl-yah ehs ehs-toh?
Do you have a...	¿Tienen una...	¿Tee-ehn-ehn oon-ah...
/smaller size?	/talla menos?	/tahl-yah meh-nohs?
/bigger size?	/talla más?	/tahl-yah mahs?
🎧 Where can I try this on?	¿Dónde están los probadores?	¿Dohn-deh ehs-tahn lohs proh-bah-dohr-ehs?
🎧 I just want to look around.	Sólo estoy mirando.	Soh-loh ehs-toy mee-rahn-doh.
I'm looking for something...	Estoy buscando algo...	Ehs-toy boos-kahn-doh ahl-goo
/more colourful.	/con más colorido.	/kohn mahs koh-lo-ree-doh.
/warmer.	/más caliente.	/mahs kah-lee-ehn-teh.
/cooler.	/más fresquito.	/mahs frehs-kee-toh.
Is this in the sale?	¿Esto está rebajado?	¿Ehs-toh ehs-tah reh-bah-khah-doh?
I'm looking for a present for...	Estoy buscando un regalo para...	Ehs-toy boos-kahn-doh oon reh-gah-loh pah-rah...
/a child.	/un niño.	/oon nee-nyoh.
/a baby.	/un bebé.	/oon beh-beh.
/my husband.	/mi marido.	/mee mah-ree-doh.
/my wife.	/mi mujer.	/mee moo-khehr.
/my friend.	/mi amigo(a).	/mee ah-meeg-oh(ah).
It doesn't fit me.	No me queda bien.	Noh meh keh-dah bee-ehn.
🎧 It's perfect.	Es perfecto.	Ehs pehr-fehk-toh.
Can you keep this for me?	¿Podría guardarme esto?	¿Pohd-ree-ah gwahr-dahr-meh ehs-toh?
If it doesn't fit, can I bring it back?	Si no me queda bien, ¿puedo devolverlo?	See noh meh keh-dah bee-ehn, ¿pweh-doh deh-bohl-behr-loh?

SHOPPING – CLOTHES AND GIFTS **43**

USEFUL WORDS – CLOTHES AND GIFTS

boutique	**boutique**	boo-teek
black	**negro**	nehg-roh
blue	**azul**	ah-thool
bra	**sujetador**	soo-kheh-tah-door
brown	**marrón**	mah-rrohn
casual	**informal**	een-fohr-mahl
chequered	**a cuadros**	ah kwahd-rohs
clothes shop	**tienda de ropa**	tee-ehn-da deh roh-pah
cotton	**algodón**	ahl-goh-dohn
earrings	**pendientes**	pehn-dee-ehn-tehs
green	**verde**	behr-deh
hat	**sombrero**	sohm-breh-roh
jacket	**chaqueta**	chah-keh-tah
jewellery	**joyas**	khoy-ahs
jumper	**jersey**	khehr-seh
necklace	**collar**	kohl-yahr
orange	**naranja**	nah-rahn-khah
receipt	**ticket**	tee-keht
red	**rojo**	roh-khoh
shirt	**camisa**	kah-mee-sah
socks	**calcetines**	kahl-theh-tee-nehs
smart	**elegante**	eh-leh-gahn-teh
swimming costume	**bañador**	bah-nyah-dohr
stripy	**a rayas**	ah rah-yas
tie	**corbata**	kohr-bah-tah
top	**camiseta**	kah-mee-seh-tah
trousers	**pantalones**	pahn-tah-loh-nehs
straps	**tirantes**	tee-rahn-tehs
underwear	**ropa interior**	roh-pah een-tehr-ee-ohr
watch	**reloj**	reh-lokh
white	**blanco**	blahn-koh
wool	**lana**	lah-nah
yellow	**amarillo**	ah-mahr-reel-yoh

SHOPPING – CLOTHES AND GIFTS

NIGHTLIFE

FINDING OUT WHAT'S GOING ON

What is there to do at night here?	¿Qué se puede hacer aquí por la noche?	¿Keh seh pweh-deh ah-thehr ah-kee pohr lah noh-cheh?
Where can I find out about...	¿Dónde puedo encontrar información sobre...	¿Dohn-deh pweh-doh ehn-kohn-trahr een-fohr-mah-thee-ohn soh-breh...
/theatres?	/los teatros?	/lohs teh-ah-trohs?
/cinemas?	/los cines?	/lohs thee-nehs?
/the opera?	/la ópera?	/lah oh-pehr-ah?
/the ballet?	/el ballet?	/ehl bah-leht?
/classical music?	/música clásica?	/moo-see-kah klah-see-kah?
What's on?	¿Qué espectáculos hay?	¿Keh ehs-pehk-tah-koo-lohs I?
When does it start?	¿A qué hora empieza?	¿Ah keh oh-rah ehm-pee-eth-thah?
When does it end?	¿A qué hora termina?	¿Ah keh oh-rah tehr-meen-ah?
Is there an interval?	¿Hay intermedio?	¿I een-tehr-meh-dee-oh?
What language is it in?	¿En qué idioma es?	¿Ehn keh ee-dee-ohm-ah ehs?
Have you seen it?	¿Lo ha visto usted?	¿Loh ah bees-toh oos-teth?
Is it good?	¿Es bueno?	¿Ehs bweh-noh?
Can you recommend a film?	¿Me podría recomendar una película?	¿Meh pohd-ree-ah reh-kohm-ehn-dahr oon-ah peh-lee-coo-lah?
Will I be able to follow the story?	¿Cree que podré seguir la historia?	¿Kreh-eh keh pohd-reh sehg-eer lah ees-tohr-ee-ah?
Is the film...	La película, ¿está...	Lah peh-lee-coo-lah, ¿ehs-tah...
/dubbed?	/doblada?	/doh-blah-dah
/subtitled?	/subtitulada?	/soob-tee-too-lah-dah?
Is there anything on in English?	¿Hay algo en inglés?	¿I ahl-goo ehn eeng-lehs?
Is there somewhere to go for a drink near here?	¿Hay algún sitio por aquí para ir a tomar una copa?	¿I ahl-goon see-tee-oh pohr ah-kee pah-rah eer ah toh-mahr oon-ah koh-pah?
Where are the best bars?	¿Dónde están los mejores bares?	¿Dohn-deh ehs-tahn lohs meh-khor-ehs bahr-ehs?

NIGHTLIFE 45

We're looking for a quiet bar	**Estamos buscando un bar tranquilo**	Ehs-tah-mohs boos-kahn-doh oon bahr trahn-kee-loh
/a lively bar.	**/animado.**	/ah-nee-mah-doh.
Is there a good gay club?	**¿Hay una buena discoteca gay?**	¿I oon-ah bweh-nah dees-koh-tehk-ah gay?
Where can we see live music?	**¿Dónde podemos ir que haya música en directo?**	¿Dohn-deh poh-deh-mohs eer keh I-yah moo-see-kah ehn dee-rehk-toh?
Do you know who's on?	**¿Sabe quién actúa?**	¿Sah-beh kee-ehn ahk-too-ah?
What sort of music is it?	**¿Qué tipo de música es?**	¿Keh tee-poh deh moo-see-kah ehs?
Are they any good?	**¿Son buenos?**	¿Sohn bweh-nohs?
What are the clubs like here?	**¿Cómo son las discotecas por aquí?**	¿Koh-moh sohn lahs dees-koh-tehk-ahs pohr ah-kee?
Does it matter what I wear?	**¿Importa el tipo de ropa que lleve?**	¿Eem-pohr-tah ehl tee-poh deh roh-pah key yeh-beh?

INVITATIONS AND SMALL TALK

Would you like to have a drink?	**¿Le gustaría ir a tomar una copa?**	¿Leh goos-tah-ree-ah eer ah tohm-ahr oon-ah koh-pah?
Shall we have something to eat?	**¿Vayamos a tomar algo de comer?**	¿Bah-yah-mohs ah tohm-ahr ahl-goh deh kohm-ehr?
What do you like to eat?	**¿Qué le apetece comer?**	¿Keh leh ah-peh-teh-theh kohm-ehr?
Which clubs do you like?	**¿Qué tipo de discotecas le gustan?**	¿Keh tee-poh deh dees-koh-tehk-ahs leh goos-tahn?
I want to go somewhere we can dance.	**Me gustaría ir a algún sitio donde podamos bailar.**	Meh goos-tah-ree-ah eer ah ahl-goon see-tee-oh dohn-deh pohd-ah-mohs bah-ee-lahr.
Shall we go there?	**¿Vamos allí?**	¿Bah-mohs ah-yee?
I thought the film was great.	**Creo que la película ha sido muy buena.**	Kreh-oh keh lah peh-lee-coo-lah ah see-doh mwee bweh-nah.

46 NIGHTLIFE

Do you know somewhere good to go round here?	¿Conoce algún sitio bueno por aquí?	¿Koh-noh-theh ahl-goon see-tee-oh bweh-noh pohr ah-kee?

ASKING FOR WHAT YOU WANT

Do you have tickets?	¿Tienen entradas?	¿Tee-ehn-ehn ehn-trah-dahs?
🎧 Can I have tickets for...	¿Podría comprar entradas para...	¿Pohd-ree-ah kohm-prahr ehn-trah-dahs pah-rah...
/tonight?	/esta noche?	/eh-stah noh-cheh?
/tomorrow?	/mañana?	/mah-nyah-nah?
/the matinee?	/la sesión de tarde?	/lah seh-see-ohn deh tahr-deh?
🎧 Could I have seats near the	¿Podrían darme asientos en las	¿Pohd-ree-ahn dahr-meh ah-see-ehn-tohs ehn lahs
/front?	/primeras filas?	/pree-mehr-rahs fee-lahs?
/the back?	/últimas filas?	/ool-tee-mahs fee-lahs?
🎧 Can I have /an ice cream? /popcorn?	¿Por favor, /un helado? /palomitas?	Pohr fah-vohr, /oon eh-lah-doh? /pah-loh-mee-tahs?

USEFUL WORDS

action	acción	ahk-thee-ohn
adventure	aventura	ah-behn-toor-ah
bar	bar	bahr
casino	casino	kah-see-noh
cinema	cine	thee-neh
club	discoteca	dees-koh-tehk-ah
comedy	comedia	coh-meh-dee-ah
exit	salida	sah-lee-dah
gay club	discoteca gay	dees-koh-tehk-ah gay
live music	música en directo	moo-see-kah ehn dee-rehk-toh
opera	ópera	oh-pehr-ah
pop	pop	pohp
rock	rock	rohk
romance	romance	roh-mahn-theh
seat	asiento	ahs-ee-ehn-toh
seating plan	plano de la platea	plah-noh deh lah plah-teh-ah
soul	soul	soh-ool
subtitled	subtitulado	soob-tee-too-lah-doh
techno	tecno	tehk-noh
ticket	entrada	ehn-trah-dah
traditional	tradicional	trah-dee-thee-ohn-ahl

NIGHTLIFE 47

HEALTH

AT THE PHARMACY

Where is the nearest pharmacy? | ¿Dónde está la farmacia más cercana? | ¿Dohn-deh ehs-tah lah fahr-mah-thee-ah mahs thehr-kahn-ah?

Is there a pharmacy open now? | ¿Hay alguna farmacia abierta ahora? | ¿I ahl-goon-ah fahr-mah-thee-ah ah-bee-ehr-tah ah-ohr-ah?

Is there an all night pharmacy? | ¿Hay alguna farmacia de guardia? | ¿I ahl-goon-ah fahr-mah-thee-ah deh gwahr-dee-ah?

Can I have this prescription please? | ¿Podría darme el medicamento de esta receta, por favor? | ¿Pohd-ree-ah dahr-meh ehl meh-dee-kah-mehn-toh deh ehs-tah reh-theh-tah, pohr fah-vohr

Can I take this when I'm pregnant? | ¿Puedo tomarme esto si estoy embarazada? | ¿Pweh-doh toh-mahr ehs-toh see ehs-toy ehm-bahr-ah-thah-dah?

I need something for... | Necesito algo para... | Neh-theh-see-toh ahl-goh pah-rah...

/a cold. | /el resfriado. | /ehl rehs-free-ah-doh.

/a headache. | /el dolor de cabeza. | /ehl doh-lohr deh kah-beh-thah.

/constipation. | /el estreñimiento. | /ehl ehs-treh-nyeem-yehn-toh.

/a cough. | /la tos. | /lah tohs.

/diarrhoea. | /la diarrea. | /lah deh-ah-rreh-ah.

/thrush. | /los hongos. | /lohs ohn-gohs.

/travel sickness. | /las náuseas. | /lahs nah-oo-see-ahs.

/toothache. | /el dolor de muelas. | /ehl doh-lohr deh mweh-lahs.

Can I have... | ¿Podría darme... | ¿pohd-ree-ah dahr-meh

/some insect repellent? | /repelente de insectos? | /reh-peh-lehn-teh deh een-sehk-tohs?

/some pain killers? | /calmantes? | /kahl-mahn-tehs?

Can I have plasters? | Me podría dar tiritas? | Meh pohd-ree-ah dahr tee-ree-tahs?

HEARING

Take one/two/three pills. | Tómese una/dos/tres pastillas. | Tohm-eh-seh oonah/dohs/trehs pahs-teel-yas.

two/three times a day.	dos/tres veces al día.	dohs/trehs beh-thehs ahl dee-ah.
/every... hours.	/cada... horas.	/kah-dah...oh-rahs.
Take with food.	Tómeselo con las comidas.	Tohm-eh-seh-loh kohn lahs kohm-ee-dahs.

AT THE DOCTOR

Is there a doctor near here?	¿Hay un médico cerca de aquí?	¿I oon meh-dee-koh thehr-kah deh ah-kee?
💿 Is there a doctor I can see now?	¿Podría ver a un médico ahora?	¿Pohd-ree-ah behr ah oon meh-dee-koh ah-ohr-ah?
💿 Is there a doctor who speaks English?	¿Hay algún médico que hable inglés?	¿I ahlg-oon meh-dee-koh keh ahb-leh eeng-lehs?
When is the surgery open?	¿Cuándo abre la consulta?	¿Kwan-doh ahb-reh lah kohn-sool-tah?
Can the doctor come here?	¿Podría venir el médico aquí?	¿Pohd-ree-ah beh-neer ehl meh-dee-koh ah-kee?
It's urgent.	Es urgente.	Ehs oor-khehn-teh.
💿 Can I see a female doctor?	¿Podría verme una doctora?	¿Pohd-ree-ah behr-meh oon-ah dohk-tohr-ah?

HEARING

What is the problem?	¿Cuál es el problema?	¿Kwahl ehs ehl proh-bleh-mah?
How do you feel?	¿Cómo se siente?	¿Koh-moh seh see-ehn-teh?
Where does it hurt?	¿Dónde le duele?	¿Dohn-deh leh doo-ehl-leh?
How long has it been like that?	¿Cuánto tiempo hace que se siente así?	¿Kwahn-toh tee-ehm-poh ah-theh keh seh see-ehn-teh ah-see?
Let me see.	Déjeme ver.	Deh-kheh-meh behr.
Please lie down.	Túmbese, por favor.	Toom-beh-seh, pohr fah-vohr.
It's not serious.	No es grave.	Noh ehs grah-beh.
You need to go to hospital.	Tiene que ir al hospital.	Tee-ehn-eh keh eer ahl ohs-pee-tahl.
Take this prescription to a pharmacy.	Lleve esta receta a la farmacia.	Yeh-beh ehs-tah reh-theh-tah ah lah fahr-mah-thee-ah.
Go to a doctor when you get home.	Vaya al médico cuando regrese a casa.	Bah-yah ahl meh-dee-koh kwahn-doh reh-greh-seh ah kah-sah.

YOUR SYMPTOMS

I'm bleeding.	Estoy sangrando.	Ehs-toy sahn-grahn-doh.
🎧 I've been vomiting.	He estado vomitando.	Eh ehs-tah-doh boh-mee-tahn-doh.
🎧 I have a fever.	Tengo fiebre.	Tehn-goh fee-ehb-reh.
Is it serious?	¿Es grave?	¿Ehs grah-beh?
I'm worried about my...	Estoy preocupado(a) por...	Ehs-toy preh-ohk-oo-pah-doh(dah) pohr...
/vision.	/mi visión.	/mee bees-ee-on.
/breathing.	/mi respiración.	/mee rehs-peer-ath-ee-ohn.
/heart.	/mi corazón.	/mee koh-rah-thohn.
It hurts here.	Me duele aquí.	Meh dweh-leh ah-kee.
I've hurt a muscle in my...	Me he hecho daño en el músculo del...	Meh eh eh-choh dah-nyoh ehn ehl moos-coo-loh dehl...
I have a pain in my...	Me duele(n)...	Meh dweh-leh(n)...
/stomach.	/el estómago.	/ehl ehs-tohm-ah-goh.
/throat.	/la garganta.	/lah gar-gahn-ta.
/chest.	/el pecho.	/ehl peh-choh.
/head.	/la cabeza.	/lah kah-beh-thah.
/legs.	/las piernas.	/lahs pyehr-nahs.
/bowels.	/la barriga.	/lah bah-rree-gah.
/kidneys.	/los riñones.	/lohs ree-nyohn-ehs.
/ears.	/los oídos.	/lohs oh-ee-dohs.
🎧 It hurts a lot...	Me duele mucho...	Meh dweh-leh moo-choh...
/when I eat.	/cuando como.	/kwahn-doh koh-moh.
/when I walk.	/cuando ando.	/kwahn-doh ahn-doh.
/all the time.	/siempre.	/syehm-preh.
/sometimes.	/a veces.	/ah beth-ehs.
/when I move.	/cuando me muevo.	/kwahn-doh meh mweh-boh.
/when I breathe.	/cuando respiro.	/kwahn-doh rehs-peer-oh.
I have...	Tengo...	Tehn-goh...
/a rash.	/un sarpullido.	/oon sahr-pool-yee-doh.
/a lump.	/un bulto.	/oon bool-toh.
/a swelling.	/una inflamación.	/oon-ah een-flah-mah-thee-ohn.

HEALTH – AT THE DOCTOR

ABOUT YOU

🔊 I am diabetic.	**Soy diabético.**	Soy dee-ah-beh-tee-koh.
I am pregnant.	**Estoy embarazada.**	Ehs-toy ehm-bahr-ah-thah-dah.
I am on the pill.	**Estoy tomando la píldora.**	Ehs-toy tohm-ahn-doh lah peel-dohr-ah.
🔊 I have….	**Tengo…**	Tehn-goh…
/asthma.	**/asma.**	/ahs-mah.
/heart problems.	**/problemas de corazón.**	/proh-bleh-mahs deh koh-rah-thohn.
/high blood pressure.	**/la tensión alta.**	/lah tehn-see-ohn ahl-tah.
I feel…	**Me siento…**	Meh see-ehn-toh
/weak.	**/débil.**	/deh-beel.
/sick.	**/náuseas.**	/nah-oo-see-ahs.
I feel cold.	**Tengo frío.**	Tehn-goh free-oh.
I feel hot.	**Tengo calor.**	Tehn-goh kahl-ohr.
I feel feverish.	**Tengo fiebre.**	Tehn-goh fee-ehb-reh.
I feel dizzy.	**Estoy mareado.**	Ehs-toy mahr-eh-ah-doh.

USEFUL WORDS

arms	**brazos**	brah-thohs
back	**espalda**	ehs-pahl-dah
birth control	**control de natalidad**	kohn-trohl deh nah-tah-lee-dath
bladder	**vejiga**	beh-khee-gah
bone	**hueso**	weh-soh
burn	**escozor**	ehs-koh-thohr
chest	**pecho**	peh-choh
condom	**condón**	kohn-dohn
cream	**crema**	kreh-mah
cut	**corte**	kohr-teh
ears	**orejas**	oh-reh-khahs
eyes	**ojos**	oh-khohs
fingers	**dedos**	deh-dohs
foot	**pie**	pyeh
gland	**glándula**	glahn-doo-lah
hand	**mano**	mah-noh
head	**cabeza**	kah-beh-thah
hips	**caderas**	kah-dehr-ahs
joint	**articulación**	ahr-tee-koo-lah-thee-ohn
knee	**rodilla**	roh-deel-yah
legs	**piernas**	pyehr-nahs
lump	**bulto**	bool-toh
muscles	**músculos**	moos-coo-lohs
neck	**cuello**	kwehl-yoh
nose	**nariz**	nahr-eeth
pelvis	**pelvis**	pehl-bees
pills	**pastillas**	pahs-teel-yahs
rash	**sarpullido**	sahr-pool-yee-doh
shoulder	**hombro**	ohm-broh
skin	**piel**	pyehl

HEALTH – AT THE DOCTOR

EMERGENCIES

sunburn	**quemadura de sol**	keh-mah-doo-rah deh sohl
swelling	**inflamación**	een-flah-mah-thee-ohn
teeth	**dientes**	dee-ehn-tehs
throat	**garganta**	gahr-gahn-tah
voice	**voz**	both

EMERGENCIES

🔊 Please help me. It's an emergency.	**Ayúdeme por favor. Es una emergencia.**	Ah-yoo-deh-meh pohr fah-vohr. Ehs oon-ah eh-mehr-khehn-thee-ah.
You must come quickly.	**Tiene que venir rápidamente.**	Tee-ehn-eh keh beh-neer rah-pee-dah-mehn-the.
🔊 I've lost my child.	**He perdido a mi hijo(a).**	Eh pehr-dee-doh ah mee ee-khoh(ah).
🔊 Call the police.	**Llame a la policía.**	Yah-meh ah lah poh-lee-thee-ah.
🔊 Call an ambulance.	**Llame a una ambulancia.**	Yah-meh ah oon-ah ahm-boo-lahn-thee-ah.
Get a doctor.	**Llame a un médico.**	Yah-meh ah oon meh-dee-koh.
They're not breathing.	**No respira.**	Noh rehs-peer-ah.
They're unconscious.	**Está inconsciente.**	Ehs-tah een-kohns-thee-ehn-teh.
They're bleeding badly.	**Está sangrando mucho.**	Ehs-tah sahn-grahn-doh moo-choh.
They have broken something.	**Se ha roto algo.**	Seh ah roh-toh ahl-goh.
Don't move them!	**¡No les mueva!**	¡Noh lehs mweh-bah!
Wait till the ambulance gets here.	**Espere a que llegue la ambulancia.**	Ehs-peh-reh ah key yeh-gheh lah ahm-boo-lahn-thee-ah.

ATTACK

Help me.	**Ayúdeme.**	Ah-yoo-deh-meh.
Please help me, I've been robbed.	**Ayúdeme por favor, me han robado.**	Ah-yoo-deh-meh pohr fah-vohr, meh ahn roh-bah-doh.
Please help me, I've been assaulted.	**Ayúdeme por favor, me han asaltado.**	Ah-yoo-deh-meh pohr fah-vohr, meh ahn ah-sahl-tah-doh.
Call the police.	**Llame a la policía.**	Yah-meh ah lah poh-lee-thee-ah.

LOSS

I'm lost.	**Me he perdido.**	Meh eh pehr-dee-doh.
I've lost my child.	**He perdido a mi hijo(a).**	Eh pehr-dee-doh ah mee ee-khoh(ah).
I've lost my…	**He perdido…**	Eh pehr-dee-doh…
/wallet	/la cartera	/lah kahr-tehr-ah
/passport	/el pasaporte	/ehl pah-sah-pohr-teh
/tickets	/los billetes	/lohs bee-yeh-tehs
/money.	/el dinero.	/ehl dee-nehr-oh.
A few minutes ago.	**Hace unos minutos.**	Ah-theh oon-ohs mee-noo-tohs.
One hour ago.	**Hace una hora.**	Ah-theh oon-ah oh-rah.
Two hours ago.	**Hace dos horas.**	Ah-theh dohs oh-rahs.
Yesterday.	**Ayer.**	Ah-yehr.

EMERGENCIES 53

MADRID – CITY ESSENTIALS

Madrid, a city of around three million people, has charm and grandeur, with wide boulevards and an old city of squares and streets.

Only selected as a capital city in the 16th century, Madrid now sprawls across over 200 square miles. It was originally a castle town, at the frontier of the Moorish empire. Today Madrid is a lively city, busy and intent on enjoying itself in bars and clubs long after other European cities have gone to bed. For visitors there are the quirky differences of culture, such as the traditional siesta – still important even in internationally-minded Madrid – and street and café life that make wandering and sightseeing a pleasure.

WHEN TO GO

August is a quiet month when Madrid's residents leave if they can. In July and August temperatures often go over 30°C. In the months of December and January it often feels close to freezing.

TOURIST INFORMATION

There are several tourist information offices; the most usefully located are at: Plaza Mayor, 3; Calle del Duque de Medinaceli 2 and at Chamartín station, Central Vestibule, Gate 16.

GETTING AROUND

Much of what you will want to see on a short trip to Madrid is within half an hour's walking of the Puerta del Sol.

If it's too hot, or too far, then public transport will get you there. If you want to go further, hiring a car in Spain is also often cheaper than in the UK.

METRO

The Madrid Metro is fast and inexpensive, and everybody uses it so it's very busy at rush hour which can last until 7.30pm on a working day. Stations are marked with a big red diamond. The Metro has ten lines – including a connection to Barajas international airport, 15 km north of Madrid central. Tickets cost a flat rate fare for all journeys, and are on sale at stations and tobacco stalls. If you intend making several journeys it's worth buying a book of ten tickets.

BUS

Buses use the same tickets as the Metro, and are a great way of seeing the sights if you're tired of walking. Most central area buses make stops in the major plazas, for instance Puerta del Sol and Plaza de Cibeles. Each stop has details of the route.

TAXI

Madrid has plenty of taxis, and they're relatively cheap by European standards. You can hail them on the street, or have your hotel or restaurant call one. The price on the meter isn't necessarily the one you will pay, as there are supplements at night, or if you leave the city limits.

CENTRAL MADRID

56 GETTING AROUND

MAP KEY
- 🟨 Places of Interest
- 🟧 Museum/Gallery
- 🟩 Park
- ⓘ Tourist Information

FINDING YOUR WAY

Like most European cities, Madrid can be a maze of unknown roads and streets that can easily confuse first-time visitors. Use this simplified map to navigate your way to some of Madrid's highlights or use it to get your bearings as you soak in the great atmosphere of this beautiful city. Not every site or place of interest falls within the illustrated area but you can easily obtain other maps from tourist information centres or even from some hotels.

GETTING AROUND

THINGS TO SEE AND DO

SHOPPING

Shopping is one of Madrid's favourite pastimes. The Puerta del Sol is a good place to start with Calle Carmen and Calle Preciados offering pedestrianised streets. South from the plaza there are antique shops, and, if it's all too much, this quarter of Madrid is also one of the best for bars and tapas food. You can find more good shopping along the Gran Via, a broad boulevard carved through the city in the 1920s and '30s.

Find high, and expensive, brand fashion in the exclusive Salamanca district, particularly Calle Serrano. For younger, and perhaps more cutting edge, designs try the area east of Plaza de Chueca.

MARKETS

Madrid's biggest flea and antique market is the busy Sunday morning El Rastro around Ribera de los Curtidores and Calle de los Embajadores. Also on Sunday morning is Mercadillo Marqués de Viana, Metro Tetuan, a smaller version of El Rastro, also with some fresh produce. Every quarter of Madrid has its daily fresh food market – one of the more colourful is San Miguel at Plaza San Miguel, Metro Puerta del Sol.

WITH CHILDREN

The zoo at Casa de Campo, from Metro Batán, is open from 10am until into the evening. Aquariums are always popular with children and Madrid's Acuario, also in Casa de Campo, will not disappoint with its great collection of fish and aquatic animals.

Opposite the Museo de America, Metro Mondoa, is the huge steel tower of Faro de Mondoa (Mondoa Lighthouse). At 92 metres you'll get stunning views of the city.

AFTER DARK

If you like staying up late, then Madrid is the place to be. One of the favourite pastimes is eating and drinking at the city's bars and cafés. As in the day, Plaza de Santa Ana is a good place for a crawl of tapas bars. Try north from Gran Via for something more edgy and sometimes seedy, with plenty of music bars and clubs. Flamenco, theatre and ballet are also available – and world-class football if you're interested. The Teatro Real, Plaza de Oriente (also known as the Teatro de la Opera) performs characteristically Spanish operas. You can also see Zarzuela, a mixture of folk tradition and high art, at the Teatro de la Zarzuela.

THINGS TO SEE AND DO

GOURMET SPECIALITIES

The red wines, such as Navarra and Rioja, and the fine cool beers are just the start of the treats in store. The Spanish also know how to make good coffee and hot chocolate.

If you want to eat there are the national favourites of paella and the cold tomato and garlic soup Sopa de Ajo. Spanish sausage – such as the red chorizo – is wonderful. Particular to Madrid is callos, or tripe, served with blood sausage and salted ham, and stews such as Cocido Madrilerio, made with sausage, bacon, vegetables and chickpeas. Air-dried ham is another delicacy. If this is something you like, the Museo del Jamón on Paseo del Prado is not to be missed.

DAY TRIPS

Monaserio de San Lorenzo de El Escorial, around 50 km north west of the city, can be reached by bus from Madrid. Begun in 1563, the palace monastery and church at the site offer amazing architectural and artistic treasures. It's busy as it is one of the most visited places in Spain.

If you have the time, try a visit to Segovia with its Roman aqueduct, old town and 11th century Alcazar.

Beautiful Toledo, which could fill a holiday on its own and is Spain's oldest town, is also just around 70 km away and can be reached by bus or train.

THINGS TO SEE AND DO **61**

MUSEUMS AND GALLERIES

Along Paseo del Prado are two of Madrid's greatest galleries. The Museo del Prado has over 100 rooms housing art from the 12th to 19th centuries, including works by El Greco and Goya. The Museo Thyssen-Bornemisza holds a large collection, which includes works by Rubens, Bernini and Caravaggio. The Museo Nacional Centro de Arte Reina´ Sofia, meanwhile, has a collection of modern art, including work by Picasso, Miró and Dalí.

Museo Arqueologico Nacional, reached from Metro Colon, is one of Madrid's most important museums, and holds art and archaeology remains from across the world. There are exhibits ranging from pre-history through to Egyptian, Roman and Renaissance art.

The Museo del Ejército (military museum), reached from Metro Banco de España, holds a huge collection of arms and armour, including the sword of El Cid. Nearby is Cason del Buen Retiro, a gallery which includes Realist and Impressionist work.

If you want to see more of Goya's work, there's the chapel he decorated with frescoes (and where he is now buried) at Ermita de San Antonio de la Florida (also known as the Panteón de Goya), reached from Metro Principe Pio.

Museo de América, Metro Moncloa, holds one of Europe's largest collections of objects and art from the Aztec, Inca, Maya and other native peoples – including beautiful gold treasure, ornaments and textiles.

Most museums and galleries are closed on Mondays.

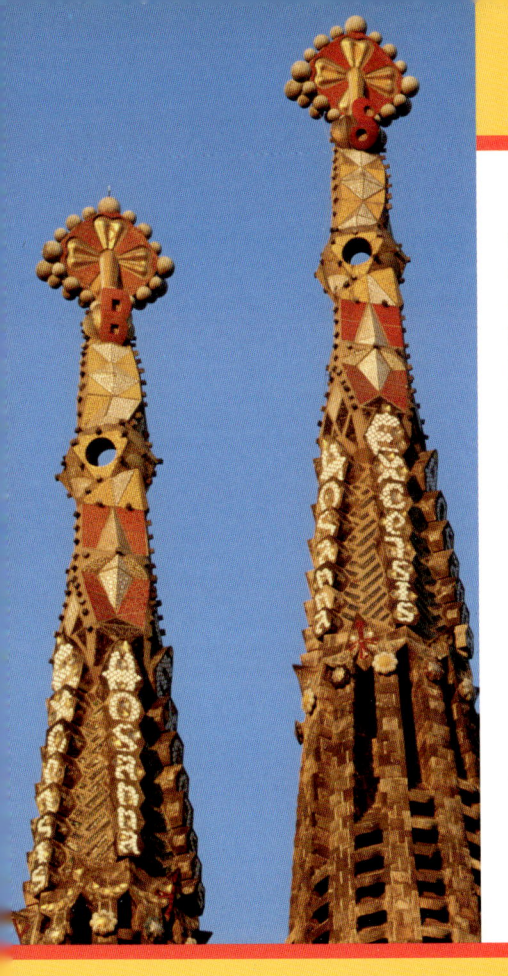

ENJOYING MADRID

Madrid's finest square is the Plaza Mayor, the old centre of business and royal life. Once a place of spectacle and execution, it is now a popular place to meet and sit, ringed by arcades of shops and cafés. South from here, down the Calle Toledo, is the old town. West from Calle Toledo you'll find the plaza and domed church of San Francisco el Grande, Spain's memorial place for the great and famous.

At the western end of Calle Mayor is the Catedral de la Virgin Almudena, the Palacio Real, the former royal palaces, and the parks and gardens of Campo del Moro, Jardines Sabatini and Jardines de las Vistallas. Whether you want to wander and relax in the sun or escape into the cool interiors of the palace and cathedral this is an unrivalled area.

From the Puerta del Sol one can follow the Carrera de San Jeronimo to the museums, gardens and open spaces of east Madrid, and the beautiful Plaza de la Cibeles and the Plaza Canovas del Castillo.

To see old Madrid, with its streets and squares, head to Plaza Santa Ana, just south east from Plaza Puerta del Sol.

PARKS AND GARDENS

Parque del Retiro is to the east of Madrid central, reached from Metro Retiro. The park offers fountains, lakes, monuments and gardens – and an escape from the traffic and noise of the city.

Casa de Campo, Metro Batan, is on the west of Madrid. Complete with cable cars and a zoo, this is a former royal hunting estate. You can swim or hire boats at the lake. To take the cable car start from Metro Argüelles. Jardin Botánico, Metro Atocha, just south of the Museo del Prado, offers a quiet haven.

Parks, architecture, galleries and fabulous nightlife are only a few of the things Madrid has to offer. Any trip to this beautiful city is sure to be the first of many – the culture and vibrancy of the place being infectious and inexhaustible.